Business Coaching Breakthrough

How To Establish Yourself, Get Clients, And Up The Odds Of Success On Your Entrepreneurial Journey

The Secret Of successful Business People
Elena Nugent

Copyright © 2020

All Rights Reserved

ISBN: 978-1-95-163081-2

DISCLAIMER AND/OR LEGAL NOTICES

While every attempt has been made to verify information provided in this book, neither the author nor the publisher assumes any responsibility for any errors, omissions, or inaccuracies. Any slights of people or organizations are unintentional. If advice concerning legal or related matters is needed, the services of qualified professional should be sought.

This book is not intended as a source of legal or accounting advice. You should be aware of any laws, which govern business transactions or other business practices in your state or province. The income statements and examples are not intended to represent or guarantee that everyone will achieve the same results. Each individual's success will be determined by his or her desire, dedication, effort, and motivation.

There are no guarantees you will duplicate the results stated in this book. You recognize that any business endeavor has the inherent risk for loss of capital. The author has no affiliation (business or personal) with any of the referenced or recommended marketing platforms, tools, systems. applications, or companies. This book contains information relating to the subject matter that is current only up to the printing date. Any reference to any persons or business, while living or deceased, existing or defunct, is purely coincidental.

Dedication

This book is dedicated to my husband Gerald, son Arseni, and Mom Nina. I love you all dearly. Thank you for helping me become the person I am today.

Acknowledgment

I want to thank my mentors and coaches – *Karl Bryan* and *Adrian Ulsh,* both are principals of Leaders Publishing Worldwide (LPW) Business Coaching Group. Your guidance and mentorship have helped me achieve unprecedented success.

About the Author

Elena Nugent is the president and owner of Results-Oriented Coaching, Training & Mentoring, LLC (www.resultsorientedcoaching.com). In addition to running her eLearning business academy and coaching company, Elena is a professional speaker and business/marketing coach who works with small-business owners to help them generate all the leads their business can handle. She knows how to double their current profits within 90 days.

Elena also coaches aspiring business/marketing coaches to help them get started, as well as to run their coaching practices with greater success.

Elena's first book, *"Instant Marketing Success, 10 New and Radical Strategies to Help Your Business Thrive"* (Leaders Publishing Worldwide, 2017), was written with small business owners in mind. It spells out fast, proven, and easy-to-implement strategies to out-perform, out-maneuver, and out-profit small business competition immediately.

Before entering the field of business coaching and digital marketing, Elena spent twenty years managing strategic marketing programs for Fortune 100 companies. As a member of their business development teams, she helped them win millions of dollars in new business. She also owned and operated small businesses – a translation and interpreting company, and a beauty salon. She has earned three Master's degrees, two in languages, and one in Business Management.

Contact Elena at info@resultsch.com to learn more about her coaching services, or visit her online business academy at www.resultsorientedcoaching.com.

Elena's personal operational beliefs are based on a person's faith to succeed, hard work, determination, self-reliance, self-sufficiency, the right attitude, optimism, and kindness to yourself and others.

Contents

Dedication i
Acknowledgment ii
About the Author iii
Introduction 1

Chapter 1 5
Business Coaching - Expectations ....

Chapter 2 8
Set Yourself up for Success ....

Chapter 3 25
Take Care of the Business Essentials ....

Chapter 4 45
Defining Your Ideal Customer, Pricing and Initial Forms ....

Chapter 5 66
Strategies for Getting Customers and Generating Growth Fast....

Chapter 6 89
Use These Long-Term Strategies to Help Scale Your Coaching Business ....

Chapter 7 139
Help Your Customers Grow with Five of the Best Business Development Strategies ....

Chapter 8 155
Use These Automation Tools to Increase Your Productivity and Improve Efficiency ....

Chapter 9...170
Establish Yourself as an Expert Authority in your Business Coaching Field..

Chapter 10...186
Learn How to Transition to Business Coaching Full-Time

Chapter 11...189
Learn the Words of Wisdom to Help You Move Forward Without Fear or Hesitation..

Chapter 12...213
Learn the Top Three Secrets of Highly Successful Business Coaches to Break Through...

Chapter 13...225
Ascend to Even Greater Success..

Page Left Blank Intentionally

Introduction

This book is my story of Business Coaching success that I would like to share with you, so you spend more time growing your business and less time learning the ropes of how to do so. This book outlines actionable strategies and tactics that, if and when implemented, will help you successfully launch, run, and grow your Business Coaching practice.

I have written this book based on my own 30+ professional experience, conversations I had with my fellow business coaches, the points I have learned from my own coaches and mentors, as well as the numerous successful business coaching training programs I took.

HOW I GOT INTO COACHING

I first got into Business Coaching when my mother suffered a stroke, and I needed to take care of her. Back then, I was working a high-profile job for a Fortune 100 company managing strategic communications and marketing. While battling with time constraints and stress, I was trying to work whole-heartedly. It was tough! Let me tell you! I began searching for ethical ways that would allow me to remain in a workforce where I could use my extensive knowledge, training, and expertise to make a more comfortable living. In addition to comfort, I was also seeking the time and flexibility to take care of my mother and my family. Business coaching gave me that.

This book is for everyone who wants to make a difference in other people's lives by teaching them how to grow their businesses while maintaining your own work schedule flexibility and making a decent revenue. You can start your Business Coaching practice part-time or full-time, depending on your goals, aspirations, time, and financial commitments.

The truth is that you only need a few hours a week to commit to coaching. You can still take care of the family or yourself plus make a good living while having this remarkable flexibility. The small business world NEEDS your knowledge and energy out there, you can and will make a handsome living, so EVERYONE wins. My goal in life now is to help others like me. I have the tools and knowledge to help those people and give them a living that wouldn't only help resolve their issues, but also help them become successful in life.

How to Use This Book

This book is divided into chapters that explain the whole process of:

1. Setting up your coaching business

2. Launching your coaching business

3. Scaling your coaching business

4. Keeping your odds of success high

You need to make sure you follow the steps in the order they are listed in the book.

Coaching assignments are provided to help you better comprehend the material and provide actions so you can start up your own coaching company as you progress reading the book. While some coaching assignments might appear time-consuming, please do not skip them - continue reading the book while working on the actions. Revisit the incomplete coaching assignments and complete them as soon as it is practical. Do not skip the assignments completely or rush through them as they provide the necessary experience to up your chances for success.

EXPERT TIP **It is important that you not implement multiple tactics or strategies all at once. Pick one or two that you feel most comfortable doing and start with those. Once you see the concepts you have picked are working, you may add more, if necessary, or just continue utilizing what's already working for you.**

Chapter 1
Business Coaching - Expectations

Business Coaching is a fairly broad term. It is a process used to take a business from where it is now to where the business owner wants it to be in the next 12 months to three years. A business coach helps a business owner to develop the best strategies for the business to achieve growth and maximum profitability in a pre-determined span of time. During that process, a business coach holds a business owner accountable, motivated, and focused on the goals set forth. A business coach is not to be confused with a consultant who usually does all the work for the client.

A business coach will meet with the business owner on a regular basis. Either weekly, biweekly, or monthly, to discuss their progress, make corrections, and keep them on track with their goals. The major problem faced by most small business owners these days is the ability to generate leads. Small businesses want leads, but few of them know how to attract customers to their business successfully. As a business coach, you will be showing the business owner how to generate more revenue using the skills and knowledge that you already have or have been taught using a business coaching training program or working with a seasoned business coach or mentor.

Is Business Coaching for You?

If you have the desire to do great for yourself and others and have a flair for business, business coaching is for you! All you need is the passion and craze to establish your own business, help companies to grow, willingness to learn, be open to being coached and mentored, and be ready to ditch the fear of success (Yes, it's not a typo!).

Chapter Summary:

1. As a business coach, you will be helping business owners to grow their businesses while earning comfortable income and maintaining your own flexible work schedule.
2. If you love helping others and have a flair for business, business coaching is for you!
3. Brainstorm with yourself and write down your expectations and estimated accomplishment dates for launching your own Business Coaching practice.

COACHING ASSIGNMENT #1:

Using the chart below, take the time to brainstorm with yourself and write down your expectations and estimated accomplishment dates for launching your own Business Coaching practice. For example:

Goal	Purpose	Due Date
Goal #1: Register my LLC	• Will help establish my business as a legal entity • Will help shield my personal assets from business liabilities	January 10, 2020
Goal #2	Expectations	Expected Achieved Date
Goal #3	Expectations	Expected Achieved Date
Goal #4	Expectations	Expected Achieved Date
Goal #5	Expectations	Expected Achieved Date

Chapter 2
Set Yourself up for Success

In this chapter, I would like to shed some light on how to prepare a proper mindset that is critical for launching a successful business coaching practice. I've also included tips on how to manage first impressions, as well as some for time management. All of this will be essential to your success as a business coach.

These are the tips I have compiled over the years that I've found most helpful. You can use them to motivate yourself and also to keep clients motivated when coaching. Keep in mind that when you have a good, correct mindset, you are more likely to make a good first impression. Having a correct mindset means envisioning yourself as an entrepreneur. Even if you're not an entrepreneur yet, you need to have that mindset.

TIPS FOR A CORRECT MINDSET
Tip #1: List Your Goals

Start by listing your goals for becoming a business coach. Use your goals as the motivating fuel to begin or continue your journey. For example, some people want a big house or expensive cars. For me, the motivation was flexibility and the ability to regulate my earnings.

Maybe you're looking for a side hustle to supplement the income you already have. Maybe you're looking to replace or exceed your current income. Maybe you'd like to become an authority in the coaching field and attain professional recognition, or even fame. Whatever your motivation is, write it down.

Tip #2: Embrace Success

You will be amazed to know how many people are afraid of being successful. They worry, *"Will I look like an imposter?"*

"Will other people listen to my advice?"

"Will my opinion sound credible?" Success is attracted to the bold and fearless, to those who are not afraid to take action. You may fall a few times while reaching your success. You may get bruised, but so what? Your success is closer than you think, and it is waiting for you. Just treat it as a normal part of your life; as something you were born

with. Period.

Tip #3: Be Prepared for Occasional Setbacks

Let's face it. Life happens. We will get tired, maybe sick occasionally. We may even have family emergencies (God forbid!).

When setbacks happen, feel free to pause and give yourself a reprieve. Then get up, dust off, and keep moving. To be successful, make yourself resilient and keep your eyes on the ultimate prize.

Tip #4: Clear Out Your Head Trash

Clear your mind to get rid of all the negativity. Ninety-nine percent of the things we worry about never happen. It's called *"head trash"* for a reason. Negativity takes you nowhere. It just takes up storage in your head. So, go ahead and get rid of it to free up some space for the thoughts and ideas that will help you become successful. To deal with anxiety, try setting aside just 5-10 minutes a day to contemplate your tasks and see what worries you the most. Try to see how real your fears are. If they are not real, ditch them. Rather than wasting time worrying, go for a walk or play with your pup. Kiss and hug your spouse or partner. Have an ice cream. Go to the movie or take a few laps in the swimming pool. Call a friend or your parents. Go sit outside and sip some coffee or a glass of wine. Get a massage or go to the spa. Meditate.

Some of the worst head trash comes from listening to other people's opinions. We are social creatures, which makes us prone to listening to judgments and taking bad advice. If you want advice on how to move forward, the best source is your mentor or coach. Don't listen to your family, coworkers, friends, or acquaintances. Just don't.

Tip #5: Find a Mentor or Coach

As an aspiring coach, who better than you should understand the importance of mentorship? If you are new to the coaching business, a mentor can help guide you. Mentors are people who have gone much farther along the same path that you are currently trying to climb. You can learn from their mistakes and reach success with fewer obstacles. If you are a seasoned coach who wants more success for yourself and your business, a coach/mentor will help you reach new heights.

Tips For Making A Good First Impression

You never get a second chance to make a first impression! First impressions can make or break a deal. And to form one only takes a few seconds. Impressions are based on your appearance, body language, dressing sense, mannerisms, and your demeanor. As a business coach, working on your first impression is a priority.

Making an excellent first impression on a client can immediately land a good deal for you. Of course, the people you are going to meet in your line of work belong to entirely different industries. Therefore, you need to make sure to prepare beforehand.

Tip #1: Research About the People That You Are Going to Meet

One of the best ways to ensure a good first impression is by knowing everything about the people you are going to meet. It shows that you are taking your clients very seriously, and people are impressed with this display of interest. It is easy enough to take a look at a prospective client's LinkedIn profile before a meeting.

Tip #2: Work on Your Appearance

How you look and carry yourself is of the utmost importance when it comes to first impressions. Take care of your hygiene and stay reasonably up to date with fashion trends. (Don't go overboard with this!) For men, a dark suit, tie, and good leather shoes are a must. You'll need to make these investments.

For women, I recommend a well-fitted suit with a skirt (no pants, please!), genuine leather shoes, quality jewelry in moderation, and neutral make-up (yes, you'll have to wear some). These are all safe bets to make a good first impression.

Tip #3: Smile

Even if you are having a bad day, make sure to wear a smile on your face for the sake of delivering an excellent first impression. If you want to have your smile complemented with whiter teeth, many teeth whitening gels are available on Amazon or at your local pharmacy. They are relatively inexpensive and provide excellent teeth whitening effect.

Tip #4: Use Confident Body Language

People tend to judge others according to their posture and body movements. Confident body language radiates positive energy, which is essential for a good first impression. Some tips for displaying confidence:

- **Stand tall:** This body language oozes confidence.

- **Make eye contact:** Confident people look at others in the eye when talking.

- **Use your hands in conversations:** People who lack confidence tend to hide their hands in a discussion. Using hand gestures shows your confidence.

Tip #5: Greet Everyone in the Room (and Remember Their Names!)

Ensure a great first impression by greeting every person that you meet. Make sure you also learn their names and use their names while addressing them. Tips to remember people's names:

1) Repeat the name soon after you hear it. For example, after Ben introduces himself, ask, *"How long have you been in this industry, Ben?"*

2) Associate the name. For example, *"Ben"* can be associated with *"Ben Affleck."*

Tip #6: Be Brief and to the Point

You want to speak clearly, and slow enough for everyone to understand. Yet you never know what mood anyone might be in when they meet you. Especially if they're having a bad day, the last thing they might want is someone taking too much of their time. Therefore, always keep your presentations precise and to the point. That way, there is no need to rush.

Tip #7: Be Entertaining

Yes, get to the point quickly. But lightening up the mood a little doesn't hurt. Try telling a joke or two to engage people in your personality. But don't go overboard! The last thing the VERY busy business owners want to see is a comedian trying to put on a show.

Tip #8: Show Appreciation

When someone agrees to a meeting, it means they have

decided to spend their time with you rather than doing something else. Show genuine gratitude for this by saying something simple such as, *"I appreciate you finding the time to meet with me. As a business coach, I'm confident that my expertise and guidance will result in your company's enormous growth and success."* Stop at that. Not a word more.

Tip #9: Don't Oversell

People have a habit of running away from sales reps. This is because they jump right in about what they have to offer. This makes them sound as if they are merely trying to sell their services. Business coaches often make this mistake, too.

Don't sound *"sales-y"* when you talk to someone about your business. Make sure that people feel like you are providing them a good value rather than selling them your services! Be specific when starting a conversation with your prospective client. Avoid using generic phrases such as *"I will show you how to increase sales"* or *"I'll show you how to become successful."*

Use numbers instead, *"Give me 45 minutes, and I'll show you how to find $20,000 in additional revenue"* or *"In 30 minutes or less, I can show you how to find $10,000 in additional revenue without spending a dime on advertising."*

Tip #10: Keep a Professional Attitude

Don't get upset if a prospective client does not want your services. Know you are not the one who is losing. They are the ones missing out on an opportunity to earn more cash for their business without spending a cent on advertising or promotion. You will find another customer. They may not be able to find another fine coach like you. It is their loss. Really.

Tip #11: Work on Your Elevator Pitch

An elevator pitch or sometimes also known as 'elevator speech' is an introduction about yourself and **the value YOU BRING TO THE CUSTOMER** to be concluded in 15 – 30 seconds. It is metaphorically called an *"elevator pitch"* because it should take no longer than it takes a person to ride the elevator to their desired floor.

By virtue of your business coaching profession, you will be meeting lots of people at networking events, one-on-one coaching sessions, focus groups, mastermind sessions, presentations, and other meetings. At these events, you will be expected to introduce yourself and briefly describe what you can do for others in the room, as well as the type of referrals you are looking for. This means that your elevator pitch must be ready at all times. If you haven't already prepared an elevator pitch, then you better start working on creating one right now.

Just remember, people care less about you and what you do. All they care about is themselves and their success. So, your elevator speech **MUST BE ABOUT THEM, NOT YOU**. Work on mastering your elevator pitch to tell your potential customer how you can benefit **THEM**. You may be surprised to hear that some people use their elevator pitch in social gatherings as well, and end up successfully fulfilling their targets.

Now that you know what an elevator pitch is, let's talk about how you can create a perfect one for yourself. **Keeping your elevator pitch concise** is the most critical part of your success with it. You need to incorporate all the highlights about you and your profession in a few sentences that can be delivered in less than 30 seconds.

Example of an Elevator Pitch:

"My name is Mary, and I'm a strategic marketing specialist. I can find any business owner a MINIMUM of $10,000 in less than 45 minutes... guaranteed... moreover, without spending a cent on marketing or advertising."

COACHING ASSIGNMENT #2: Learn your *"elevator pitch"* and practice it several times until you are completely satisfied with your confidence level and delivery.

Time Management Tips

When starting your journey towards building a successful business or company, time management is key. At first, managing everything at once can be quite tricky. Keep in mind that everything can be achieved with enough effort and proper planning.

Here are the time management tips that work for me:

1. Create and follow a schedule for your daily routine (YES, EVEN IF YOU WORK FROM HOME!).

2. Plan your activities and projects around your energy level — for example, my productivity peaks between 8am-12 pm, then again between 8pm-10pm. So, I try to tackle high priority/most complex projects around those times while leaving menial tasks for other times.

3. Set aside time for contingencies and interruptions, such as family time, doctors' appointments, lunch breaks, time on social media, and visiting friends.

4. Take at least 15 minutes daily to prepare a schedule for the next day (preferably before you retire for the night).

5. Set goals for each day and make sure you achieve them before going to bed.

6. Wake up every day with positive energy and always hope for a good day.

7. Meditate daily, immediately after waking up if possible. If not, find just 10 minutes out of your busy schedule. Find a place where you can sit

comfortably and start a mediation application on your smartphone. You will feel so much better after those 10 minutes that it is not even funny.

8. If you get distracted during work, take a break. Leave your desk and do some physical activity (go for a walk or call a friend) to refresh your mind. When you feel refreshed, get back to work.

9. Focus on one thing at a time to avoid feeling overwhelmed.

10. Mute your personal social media. Social media platforms are great for marketing uses. However, cutting personal social media from your life will free up much needed time for developing yourself into a great business/marketing coach.

11. Remain prepared for occasional setbacks in your life such as illnesses, fatigue, lack of sleep, and even situational depression. Plan your schedule accordingly.

Keep Your Eye on the Prize

In conclusion, as you begin your journey, stay laser-focused on what you want to achieve. If you set time to send out a few promotional e-mails to your potential customers, but you choose to browse Facebook instead, then you have a problem on your hands. It's called distraction. It's important that you manage your time to stay the course. Morning affirmations or daily focus and concentration meditations help me immensely in keeping on track.

Once you start networking and meeting with clients, never underestimate the value of making a good first impression. As it's said, *"the first impression is the last impression."* Although I do believe that a bad first impression can be remedied, later on, I suggest that you don't take that chance. Make sure there are adequate preparations, to make, not break, your image in the mind of any potential customers.

And remember to always keep in mind why are you doing this. Determine your personal goals, as well as the *"why"* you present to clients. Clear your mind of all negativity, embrace success, and be ready to persevere. A coach or mentor will also be a key asset on your journey going into business for yourself.

You will go through disappointments, sickness, lack of motivation, distractions, denial—you name it! Remember, all this is perfectly normal. Please take it as is and MOVE ON. Keep your eyes on the prize. It's closer and more achievable than you think. Now that you have your mindset for success, in the next chapter, we will look at determining your ideal customer and thinking about your potential niche, as well as some important forms for getting started with clients.

Chapter Summary

1. Develop a proper mindset as it is critical for launching a successful business coaching practice.

2. Learn and practice how to make a good first impression.

3. Perfect and learn your elevator pitch that would describe what value you bring to the customers. Your elevator pitch must be about YOUR CUSTOMERS, NOT YOU.

4. Learn and start implementing your time management strategy to help you stay on track and

prevent burnout and fatigue.

5. Always keep your eyes on the prize.

Complete Coaching Assignment #3 to get more clarity on what prevents you from starting your own business coaching practice.

COACHING ASSIGNMENT #2: a) Identify all your motivational factors for starting your coaching business. List them in the LEFT column. b) Identify all the obstacles and list them in the CENTER column. c) Outline solutions to overcome the obstacles in the third column. Use the tips in this chapter to help you find solutions.

I Want to Start My Own Consulting Business Because…	The things that Prevent Me from Starting My Own Consulting Business are…	I Can Overcome these Obstacles by…

I Want to Start My Own Consulting Business Because...	The things that Prevent Me from Starting My Own Consulting Business are...	I Can Overcome these Obstacles by...

Chapter 3
Take Care of the Business Essentials

Before you start coaching clients, you need to set yourself up as a business. To set up your business, follow the steps outlined in this chapter. Think of it like you're a pilot going through your preflight checklist. Every item on the checklist is there to ensure best practices, prevent crashes, and so on.

The pilots don't question any item on that list. They just do it. They check, check, check, and then take off. You can do the same thing with the information presented here. I have even included a checklist for you at the end of the chapter.

Step 1: Set up a Correct Legal Structure

Any business needs an appropriate legal structure. Business coaching has a similar requirement. Following are some fundamental legal structures that you can choose:

- Sole Proprietorship

- Limited Liability Company (LLC)
- Partnership
- Corporation

Before making your decision on the legal structure to choose, please consult a Certified Professional Accountant (CPA) or a lawyer to decide what's best for you. Check with your state and local county rules and regulations to see what else you need to do to register your business to operate as a legal entity.

Sole Proprietorship

If you are the only owner of your business, then the best legal structure to choose is a sole proprietorship. A sole proprietorship is the most straightforward business structure to set up. It requires the least paperwork, and it is also one of the least expensive choices. However, as the sole owner of a business, you are responsible for all debts and liabilities that your business incurs. You will have to bear losses single-handedly if your business hits rough patches.

Limited Liability Company (LLC)

Limited Liability Company or LLC is one of the best legal structures to go for when looking to set up your business. You can protect your assets in this structure. If your business faces any litigation or suffers a loss, you will only lose whatever your business holds as assets.

Partnership

The partnership consists of more than one owner. This legal structure means that you can share all your expenses, profits, and losses with your partner/s. However, I always recommend that you choose your partners very carefully since many businesses close their doors due to a fallout between the partners.

A partnership business is based on a partnership deed. Legally speaking, the deed contains ownership rights, profit percentages, and different rules that partners create to keep the business operational. Make sure that your partnership deed is well-formed, and all partners agree to all the terms before commencing your business.

Corporation

The corporation is by far the most complex legal structure that you can choose for your business. The most significant advantage of forming a corporation is a limited liability for all the stockholders. However, the overall setup is just too expensive to justify this one benefit. In the coaching business, this type of legal structure may not be very suitable unless you have several stakeholders with you that are willing to take this kind of risk.

Step 2: Pick a Company Name and Domain Name that WORK

One of the most important decisions that you will be required to make is choosing your company's name. Make sure that the company name that you are choosing hasn't already been taken in order to avoid any copyright battles.

The next obvious step is to choose a domain name. The best way to do that is by going to . Make sure that the domain name related to your company is available. You can even select the company name based on the available domain names. It is always wise to check the availability of the domain name before selecting your company name.

For business coaching, domain names, including *"action"* or active words, work best. For example, *"action-focused-coaching," "take-action-now", "make-profit-now,",* etc.

Once you have registered your company's name, there is no going back!

Step 3: Set up a Business E-Mail

After registering your company and domain name by going to www.godaddy.com, you need to set up a business e-mail from the services offered by the same site. A business e-mail makes your company look professional.

A personal e-mail address doesn't work well. People have a more difficult time trusting a business coach who has a public domain e-mail account. For example, if your domain name is www.abcbusiness.com, then your e-mail address should be ceo@abcbusiness.com.

Having a sound e-mail signature is a MUST. Take this example:

"Best Regards,

Your Business Coach John Doe"

This is a great start, but it does not deliver a real message.

Use the following template to create your personalized e-mail signature:

Dedicated To Your Business Success!

John Doe

I help Businesses Thrive

Business Coach/ Market Strategist / Author / Speaker

Owner, Name of Your Company

OR

Give me 45 minutes, and I will show you how to generate $100,000 in additional revenue for your business without spending a dime on advertising.

555-444-33-22

jdoe@yourcompanyname.com

www.yourWebsite.com

Step 4: Create a Website

A Website represents the identity of any business online. It offers prospective clients a convenient way to access the company and its services. It gives a face to the business. Create a Website for your business coaching services so people can identify you among the many other business coaches. When populating your website with content, make sure you have a message of what value you provide to your ideal customer. Provide metrics of what you are capable of delivering to your customers such as a timeframe (*"Give me 30 days, and I'll show you how to generate $20,000 in additional revenue"*), expected results (*"I will show you how to double your revenue in six months"*), etc.

Step 5: Obtain an Employee Identification Number (EIN)

The next most important thing to do after setting up the business e-mail and Website is to obtain an EIN for your company. The EIN is simply a nine-digit number that is assigned by the U.S. Internal Revenue Service (IRS) to all the businesses that operate in the United States. This number serves as an identification for each business entity. It is like a social security number for your business. You can get the EIN for your company at www.irs.gov/businesses.

Step 6: Create an Online Payment Processing

Account

Once you have your EIN, it is time to create a PayPal Business account for your business. You can do that by visiting www.paypal.com. Choose *"Business"* and follow the steps outlined for creating a business account. You can also visit https://stripe.com. Stripe can also be helpful when it comes to accepting payments online.

Step 7: Set up an Accounting / Payroll System

To manage your company's finances and accounting, you will need professional accounting software. It will help you track your expenses, pay your employees or contractors, if necessary, and support filing your company's taxes. The accounting software these days is so intuitive that you will most likely not need a Certified Professional Accountant (CPA) to do accounting and payroll for you unless you decide otherwise.

For your accounting software purposes, I would recommend:

- Intuit Quickbooks (https://quickbooks.intuit.com/)

- A Cloud-based Freshbooks (https://www.freshbooks.com/)
- Zoho Books (https://www.zoho.com/books/)

I personally have been using Intuit Quickbooks for a number of years now, and I'm quite happy with it. Do the feature comparison of these three systems and see which one suits your business needs and wallet best.

Step 8: Take a Professional Photograph

Now that you have set up your Website with your company's name and e-mail, you should display a photograph of yourself on your Website so your potential customers can identify you. Make sure you show a friendly face!

I recommend using a professional camera. Stand against a white background, and wear a dark suit. Women should wear minimum jewelry. Moderate make-up is a safe option. Remember, this photo is going to be the FACE of your business. Hire a professional photographer if necessary.

If you are not satisfied with your photo, then you can get it retouched by a professional photo editor at the Fiverr

Website (www.fiverr.com) for $5.

Step 9: Create and Print Business Cards

The next thing you need to do is create business cards for yourself and your employees (if applicable). If you are looking for a minimum investment with high quality, go to www.vistaprint.com.

To ensure your business card makes a lasting impression on your customers, it must provide more than just your name and website. Your business card must carry a message of your value. I recommend the following template for your business card:

FRONT:

John Doe

Success Coach / Business Growth Expert

I DO BUSINESS MAKEOVERS

Want to make $100,000 in additional revenue in only 20 days? I will show you how.

YOUR COMPANY'S NAME

E-mail

Phone:

Website URL:

BACK
- *I will show you how to generate all the leads you can handle*
- *Never spend a dime on marketing and advertising*
- *Double your current profits within three months*

Step 10: Open a Business Bank Account for Your Business

You need to open a business account with the bank of your choice for accounting and tax purposes. Many banks offer *"Open Business Account"* as an option of online banking package. Some banks still require you to pay them a visit in person to complete the required paperwork. So, visit your bank Website or call them to explore your options before proceeding.

Business Tip: Do your best to cultivate a good relationship with your banker. As a business coach, you may be asked to provide coaching or training for the small business owners who also bank there.

Step 11: Set up a Cloud-Based Telephone System

Avoid using your personal phone for business purposes in order to keep your personal and business life separate. To set up a Cloud-based telephone system, visit

www.vonage.com or www.ringcentral.com.

Step 12: Register for a Web Conferencing Service

The next thing you need to do after setting up the cloud-based telephone service is register for an excellent Web conferencing service. The best places to get Web conferencing service according to my personal experience are https://www.join.me/ or www.startmeeting.com.

Additional Web Conferencing platforms include Time Trade (https://www.timetrade.com/), Zoom (https://www.zoom.us/?utm_source=zoom.com), and many others. Just go ahead and do the free trial of the platforms you like and see which one best fits your needs.

Step 13: Find and Sign up with a Proven E-Mail Marketing/Customer Relationship Management (CRM) Platform

After setting up all the important stuff related to your business, the next obvious thing to do is promote your business by targeting your potential clients. The best and most professional way to contact your potential clients is through e-mail marketing. Sign up for an e-mail marketing service to help you reach your target audience.

You can sign up for a great e-mail marketing platform by visiting www.aweber.com. Aweber is an affordable and extremely easy-to-use e-mail marketing platform that I highly recommend.

Step 14: Buy a P.O Box

If you don't want to use your home business address for official business mail, I recommend that you buy a P.O Box at your local post office. The U.S. CAN-SPAM Act requires that when sending ads via e-mail, you tell your recipients where you are located.

If you are going to work from home, I bet you don't want to disclose your home address. However, according to the CAN-SPAM Act, *"your message **must** include your valid physical postal address. This can be your current street address, a post office box you've registered with the U.S. Postal Service, or a private mailbox you've registered with a commercial mail receiving agency established under*

Postal Service regulations." So, get a P.O. Box and register it as the address to be displayed in your ad e-mails. P.O. Box service would cost you between $30-$40 a month, depending on the state you live in.

These days, many business incubators or shared workspace business facilities (the so-called *"co-working facilities"*) offer *"look real"* business addresses that you can buy as the *"official"* business address for your company. This will have an actual street name and building number, just like any other address. The only difference is it works as a P.O. Box. Only you will know that. This service costs between $50 to $150 a month depending on the state you live in.

Should you decide to go with this option, Google *"office space sharing or co-working facilities," "business incubators,"* in your area, and contact them to get more details on obtaining a *"look real"* business mailing address. Decide for yourself what works for you, whether it is a P.O. Box or a *"Look Real"* business address.

Step 15: Buy General Liability Insurance

I would recommend that you buy general liability

insurance as a Business Coach. It is fairly low-cost and will provide you peace of mind from a general liability perspective. One of the insurance companies I recommend is Biberk at https://www.biberk.com/.

Step 16: Secure an Office Space (if necessary)

You can run your Business Coaching practice from the comfort of your own home, providing you have a room available to set up your work station and conduct coaching sessions virtually via Skype or by phone. If, for some reason, you can't work from home, there are low-cost options available for you out there. One of them is a Share Desk (https://www.sharedesk.net/).

Share Desk allows you to find a space to meet or work, and book it online. You can book a conference room, an office or simply a desk. ServeCorp is another coworking solution that, in addition to office space or desk, offers bilingual receptionists, landline phones, *"look-real"* addresses, printing/faxing service, and much more. Another comparable service is offered by Davinci Virtual at https://www.davincivirtual.com/. I recommend that you review all options available and decide which one works best for you. Pick what will best help you stay productive and provide quality service to your customers. The business set-up recommendations I provided above are sufficient to get you started in the Business Coaching practice. You would certainly need to evaluate your progress as you move along and tweak the tools and platforms as necessary.

Perform Search Engine Optimization (SEO)

Having a Website is great, but if your potential customers can't see or find it, it's useless. Your site will need Search Engine Optimization (SEO) to ensure it ends up in front of potential customers. SEO will get you more leads and more inquiries about your services. The following instructions will guide you through doing the SEO for your site.

Add Your Website URL to Google

Method-1: Submit Your URL Directly Through Google

Open the Google search engine Home page (https://www.google.com/) and click the **Business** link at the bottom.

Method-2: Use Submit Express to Add Your URL to Multiple Search Engines

Visit the Submit Express Website (http://www.socialsubmissionengine.com/) if you want to add your URL to Google as well as other search engines such as Yahoo, Bing, and many others.

Method-3: Use My Submitter

1. Go to My Submitter homepage (http://www.mysubmitter.com/).

2. Enter your URL in the URL field and your e-mail address in the textbox designated for e-mail.

In conclusion, get started setting up your business! Get your company name and domain set up, and start working on your legal structure. Try out some different Web-based telephone and conferencing systems to see what might work best for you.

Chapter Summary:

To have a reputable business, you will need to create a legal entity of your choice. I highly recommend that you choose LLC. This type of legal entity will help you protect your personal assets, if necessary. Please feel free to review other types and pick the one that suits you best. To operate a business effectively and efficiently, you will need to set it up using various platforms and tools. These include:

- Picking the action-driven company's name
- Setting up a business e-mail
- Creating your company's Website
- Having EIN generated
- Setting up online payment processing
- Setting up a payroll system
- Taking a professional photograph of yourself
- Creating Business cards
- Opening a Business Bank account
- Having a cloud-based telephone system
- Setting up a Web-conferencing service
- Setting up a CRM system
- Buying a P.O. Box (optional)

- Buying a General Liability Insurance (Optional)
- Renting a business space (Optional)

COACHING ASSIGNMENT #3: Use the checklist below to set up your Business Coaching practice. This checklist will help you stay on top of the business essentials.

Action #	Description	Due Date	Status (Completed/In-progress/Closed)
1.	Pick my company's name		
2.	• Register company's domain • Create a professional business e-mail		
3.	Form my business and file all the necessary paperwork with my state and county government		
4.	Set up my business Website		
5.	Obtain my company's EIN		
6.	Create a Business PayPal Account (and Stripe)		
7.	Set up an accounting system		
8.	Have a professional photo of myself		

BUSINESS COACHING BREAKTHROUGH

Action #	Description	Due Date	Status (Completed/In-progress/Closed)
	taken		
9.	Create and print business cards		
10.	Open a Business bank account		
11.	Set up a Cloud-based telephone service		
12.	Set up a Web conferencing service		
13.	Set up a CRM system		
14.	Buy a P.O. Box		
15.	Buy a general liability insurance		
16.	Secure an office space (if necessary)		

Chapter 4
Defining Your Ideal Customer, Pricing, and Initial Forms

What is *"The Ideal Customer?"*

Simply said, the *"ideal customer"* is the client or customer who will most benefit from your service or offering. If you know who your ideal customer is, this will up your chances for business success. You can plan a marketing strategy that is adequately adjusted to that particular segment of customers without wasting your hard-earned dollars on *"broad"* marketing campaigns unlikely to yield results. This is why it is crucial for you to identify and define the common traits of your ideal client.

The idea of your perfect client sets a few things straight for you before you even begin your business. It helps you understand the size of the business you should go for, the niche you need to gain expertise in, and the compensation you should charge for your services. When I first got started, I targeted small, local businesses. As a former small business owner, I knew exactly what they were going through and the kind of help they needed.

I wanted to help them avoid the mistakes that I've made. I related to local small businesses very well. So, I started attending networking events and getting in touch with the local small businesses. I knew exactly what their pain points were and their struggles. That was my ideal customer. As a business coach, your overall clients are business owners. You need to decide for yourself on the ideal size of the business you want to target – whether it is small to medium-size.

I recommend small business (those that generates up to $1,000,000 in sales annually). This is because small businesses make up the majority of all companies in the U.S. and internationally, and also because small business owners ALWAYS struggle with lead generation. So, small business owners NEED you.

To Niche or Not to Niche

Business coaches often start by trying their luck on different niches until they finally find one that they are the most comfortable with. Start with the niche that you have experience working in previously. For example, targeted clients in the hotel industry if you have worked in the hotel business before. Businesses in this niche are then your ideal customer. Some of my fellow business coaches have been successful chiropractors, business brokers, restaurant owners, hair salon owners, and even car dealers in the past. Now they specialize in the fields where they are experts: Chiropractors, restaurants, hair salons, etc. They put their institutional knowledge of the subject businesses to work in addition to marketing and other business-related disciplines.

EXPERT TIP **Having an institutional knowledge is not a requirement, however. You can still pick an industry niche, or you can specialize in the businesses based on their size or sales volume. All you need is the willingness to put your energy, knowledge, expertise, and passion toward helping those businesses out.**

Decide on Your Coaching Fees

Of course, one of the most important things to consider as a professional business coach is to decide how much you want to charge your customers for your services.

When it comes to business coaching, success mostly depends on consistency in this field. As a business coach, your main goal is to keep your customers on track by making sure their goals and commitments are achieved. They should start seeing more revenue coming in as a result of your coaching.

Create strategies to tackle any obstacles between the customers and their goals. The best way to make sure that you and your customers are on the right track is by tracking your progress as you advance towards the next level of coaching. The structure of your coaching program immensely depends upon your offering in general and the coaching services that you offer in particular.

For example, for me, a broke business is not an ideal customer. As much as I love helping people, I have bills to pay. But I know a fellow coach who works with struggling businesses. She signs them up in her business academy for $99 a month. She meets with them on the phone every other month to check in on them. Then, once they start generating cash based on those e-video lessons that she provides to them through her e-business academy, she upgrades them to a higher package.

The best way to decide on your coaching fee is by developing a set of coaching packages that you offer to the business owners. This way, your customers will have the flexibility to choose the package that fits their financial situation. With multiple options open to your clients, they are more likely to meet at least one of your asking prices.

It is not uncommon for business coaches to earn a profit share from the profits generated as a result of their business coaching. Profit-sharing can range from 10percent-25percent, as agreed upon between the business coach and the business owner prior to starting working together. Should you decide to go into profit-sharing with a business owner, you must consult your attorney and have him write the so-called Contingency Agreement for you based on your specific situation, terms, conditions, and laws of the state you are in.

Remember to offer a *"graduated payment"* option to your customers. This provides payment flexibility for them and helps you attract and retain more customers.

EXPERT TIP: I would also highly recommend that you never use a la carte prices. You need to package your services and sell them as a package. If a client only wants to pay by session and only pays for three, who wins? Nobody. Because no matter how small the business is, the business owner needs to work with a coach for at least 12 months in order to see the results. That's why a la carte price is not going to work. It has to be a 12-month commitment at the least.

The table below serves as a reference for you to develop your own pricing packages.

Coaching Package Level	Items Included	Price

BUSINESS COACHING BREAKTHROUGH

Coaching Package Level	Items Included	Price
Level 1 (Platinum)	<ul><li>Weekly 1-1 coaching calls</li><li>Access to online resources</li><li>Access to the Facebook Mastermind Group</li><li>Access to Weekly Group Coaching</li><li>Unlimited e-mail support</li></ul>	$997-$5000 monthly
Level 2 (Gold)`	<ul><li>Monthly 1-1 coaching calls</li><li>Access to Facebook Mastermind Group</li><li>Access to Weekly Group Coaching</li><li>Access to online resources</li></ul>	$497-$997 monthly
Level 3 (Silver)	<ul><li>One 1-1 coaching call at the beginning</li><li>Access to online resources</li><li>Access to the Facebook Mastermind group</li></ul>	$99-$197 monthly
Coaching Scholarship	<ul><li>Monthly 1-1 coaching</li><li>Access to the Facebook</li></ul>	$5000 Annually (paid as a lump sum)

Coaching Package Level	Items Included	Price
	Mastermind Group • Access to the weekly group coaching • Access to online resources	
Start-up* (once the "start-up" starts generating profits, I recommend that you upgrade them to a level that would provide them the best value)	• One 1-1 coaching at the beginning • Access to the Facebook Mastermind Group • Access to online resources	$0 – first month $99 -second month and beyond until they start generating profits.

You can mix and match the items from your packages and offer them for sale. For example, you can sell your group coaching offering to the customer for six to 12 months to ensure they reap the maximum benefits of it.

IMPORTANT FORMS
Business Initial Assessment Form

Use a sample Business Initial Assessment Form below to get initial information from your customers. Feel free to add more questions, as necessary based on your perspective customer. This information should help you determine the best strategy for them, as well as the best pricing structure.

This form will help you see what companies need help with. You will want to keep your ideal customer and your particular expertise in mind when formulating your questions. Below are some example questions to use on a Business Initial Assessment Form. You may need to include other areas, depending on your focus and expertise, but this will be a good start.

1. How does the product/services offered **differ** from your competitors?

2. Do you have a **Website**?

3. What **marketing materials** are you using to promote your business?

4. What **marketing media** do you use to promote your business?

5. How would you describe these marketing media? Do they **effectively reach** your target clientele?

6. How much do you spend on your **marketing campaigns**?

7. Would you describe these marketing media as **effective** in reaching your core target market?

8. How big is your clientele?

9. In terms of profit, what area of your venture is most **profitable**?

10. In terms of transactions, what are your **average sales value** for every transaction?

11. What is your **average gross profit percentage** for every transaction?

12. What number of **inquiries** do you receive every day/week/month?

EXPERT TIP Some customers may not be willing to provide you all the information you ask for as part of a business assessment. Be gentle but firm by responding that you won't be able to help them without the information you are requesting.

The Coaching Agreement

After getting the Business Initial Assessment Form out of the way, the next most important thing to do is signing a coaching agreement with your customer. You are going to spend more than a few hours together, which will only work through mutual respect and trust between both parties. An agreement helps ensure that both of you are on the same page.

The best way to make sure that there are no misunderstandings regarding the services that you are going to offer is by signing an agreement. Create a contract that stipulates all your services and also the terms and conditions of the contract. You can use the sample Coaching Agreement below as a model for the one you create for your business.

Insert Company Name 12-Month Agreement:

Business Name:

Invoice No:

Contact Name:

Invoice Date:

BUSINESS COACHING BREAKTHROUGH

Business Address:

Agreement

With the completion of this 12-month agreement and at acceptance by *[insert company name]*, *[insert company name]* agrees to provide the business, whose details are stated above, without limitations with the following:

Product/Service	Price	GST	Total
		Total:	
		Minus Deposit:	
		Balance Due:	

Method of Payment:

Credit Card	Visa	Other	Check
		Master Card	Bankcard	Finance

BUSINESS COACHING BREAKTHROUGH

Number on Card ☐☐☐☐ ☐☐☐☐ ☐☐☐☐ ☐☐☐☐

Expiry Date ☐☐ ☐☐

Name on Card

Signature on Card

In conclusion,

Payment Terms (if applicable):

Authorization

Would you like to receive information from [*Insert Licensee company name*] about any new Products or special offers as and when they become available?

Yes ☐   No ☐

Important Acknowledgement

Before signing this agreement, I have read, understood, and agreed to be bound by the terms and conditions of this Agreement.

Print Name: Position:

Authorizing Signature: Date:

Terms and Conditions of Agreement

1. Definitions

The terms listed below shall bear the following meanings:

"Customer" means the business whose details are written at the beginning of this Agreement. *"Coach"* means the

company that goes into the Agreement to provide the Customer the services, and is an authorized licensee of ABC Coaching. *"Services"* simply refers to the coaching services that have been bought from the coach by the Customer.

2. **Supply of Goods and S**
3. **ervices**

The Coach agrees to provide the Customer with the Products as written on the front of this Agreement, subject to Clause 3 below. The Customer is aware and admits knowledge that it may require additional services from the Coach for extra costs, supplying of these services shall be at the discretion of the Coach.

4. **Termination by Coach**

This Agreement may, without notice, be immediately terminated if the Customer fails to adhere to the terms of payment clearly stated on the front of this Agreement, or a failure by the Customer to remedy the breach of contract within 14 days of receiving written notification of the breach and a notification that it has been remedied. In this event, the Coach terminates this Agreement; the Coach reserves the sole authority to repossess the Products.

5. Information

The information, as stated in the Products, is for reference only. The sale of the Products on the understanding of the following terms:

(1) The Coach would not be held responsible for the outcome of any actions taken based on information found in the Services, nor for any mistakes or error by omission from the Products; and

(2) The Coach is not obligated to engage in providing legal, accounting, professional, or other advice or services. The Coach hereby places a disclaimer on all liability and cannot be held responsible for any person, be it a buyer or reader of this publication or not, in respect of anything, and of the outcome of anything, done or omitted to be done by any such person in reliance, whether totally or partially, upon the whole or any part of the items contained in the services.

6. Performance

None of the two parties involved shall be held responsible for delays or the inability to perform due to acts beyond human control, such as the acts of God, acts of war, epidemics, riot, civil insurrection, power outages, fire, earthquakes, and other disasters.

7. Disclaimer

The Customer is of the knowledge of and agrees that the Coach and any agent, employee, or anyone representing the Coach are not making any promises or guarantees as regards the income, revenue, or profits which might or can be earned by the Customer by using the information stated in the Services. The outcome recorded by the Customer is primarily dependent on the Customer's own ability to apply and interpret the information in the Services.

8. Proper Law

This agreement shall be interpreted in accordance with the laws of the state of ABC and that the law of the state of ABC shall be the proper law guiding this agreement.

9. Results

Results are as money, motivation, progress, marketing plan, business plan, the structure of the business, thought-provoking conversation, changes and altering of business practices, time management improvements, regular correspondence, and a deeper understanding of how businesses can be sold to target markets.

10. 100percent Money-Back Guarantee

About the conditions stated below – the training program is completed as instructed by our professionals in following the schedule and completing the workbook – if you have not gotten desired results, you are guaranteed a full refund of all the money that you have paid to the Coach for the training program under this Agreement. (You may also want to add 30 or 90-day reviews and base the money-back guarantee within each interval).

11. Conditions:

1. This guarantee will be considered void in situations as follows:

(a) You did not **finish** your twelve-month training program and at all times made a genuine and earnest attempt to implement the program;

(b) You have not **turned in your completed workbook** to the Coach every month;

(c) You had not made payment of funds to the Coach as and when were due;

2. Your money-back guarantee is with an exception to fees, interest payments, late charges, or any charges your bank applies to you to the refund initiated.

In conclusion, every industry has a concept of an ideal customer or client. This is no different in the field of business coaching. Think about what skills you can offer and what types of businesses might best benefit. Consider your profit, as well. Once you have determined your ideal client, you can go ahead and set up your initial forms. In the next chapter, I'll step you through the strategies to generate leads.

Chapter Summary:

1. Define your ideal customer by deciding what kind of businesses will benefit best from your services and expertise. You should decide if you want to work with small or large businesses and what value you are going to bring to that business.

2. Decide if you want to work with a certain niche — for example, beauty salons only or restaurants. Having an institutional knowledge in a certain area is definitely a plus but not a requirement.

3. Package and sell your services as various packages with a 12-month commitment from the customer to allow them to benefit from your services for a maximum benefit.

4. Strive to have a signed Coaching Agreement with your client. It is critical to ensure there is no misunderstanding between you and the business owner regarding the services you are offering.

Coaching Assignment #4:

Determine your ideal customer. Think about your experience and what areas you might be able to best help business owners. Decide if a niche seems right for you. Then put together your own Business Initial Assessment Form, Pricing Schedule, and Business Agreement Form.

Chapter 5
Strategies for Getting Customers and Generating Growth Fast

EXPERT TIP

Growing your business coaching practice takes serious time and commitment. Be consistent in your effort, and the revenue will follow.

This chapter explains how to start generating cash while you are working to implement your strategic marketing steps. You need to establish yourself and promote your practice, but you also need to start making money.

So, first, take the tactical steps to get a foot in the door fairly immediately. Secondly, design a strategy to grow your practice by aligning your long-term goals with the value you are bringing to your customers. You will need to seek out local opportunities, and show clients that you know your stuff.

Continue reading to learn proven marketing strategies for getting your first ten customers FAST.

Strategy #1: Form a Joint Venture (JV) with a Local Business Services Provider(s)

Forming a JV with a trusted business services provider is one proven method to generate leads for your business. People who have been working in services for a long time have many connections among their clients or partners. They also have a positive image and reputation that you can use to your benefit. A Joint Venture allows you to align yourself with someone who holds a trustworthy position in the service industry. This person can be a Certified Professional Accountant (CPA), a tax advisor, a printer, a banker, or a business broker.

You can find these trusted service providers near your business place. Invite them over for a cup of coffee to discuss a possible partnership with them. If they are not available to meet face-to-face, a simple e-mail or a phone call works just fine. If you don't know a business provider personally, you can find them on the Internet, Yellow Pages, www.alignable.com, and many other business directories or business networking portals. When choosing a JV partner, you have to keep a systematic and intelligent approach. Find someone who has a broad reach. Evaluate the profile of each of the people you are considering. Determine if they will be able to give you sufficient leads. Aim at building long-term cooperation with those business providers since it is mutually beneficial for both of you. Make sure they understand that you are looking for a long-term partner and that your goal is to help local businesses grow.

If you can't meet with your potential JV partner in person, I suggest you start with a phone call to be followed up by an e-mail. It is crucial that you keep it sweet and short and not sound *"sales-y."* Here is a sample e-mail you can use to send to a service provider or use it as a script for your phone call:

Hi John,

My name is Samantha Jones, and I am a Business Coach. I help local businesses grow and expand by teaching them how to implement the best promotional practices without spending a dime on advertising. I am looking for local business owners who would like to benefit from my training services. I am also looking for a sponsor to support my Marketing Bootcamp. If you are interested, let's set up a meeting and discuss it in more detail. Sound good?

Once you have set up a partnership, make sure your JV partner sends out the announcements about your training opportunities to his/her database of clients, highlighting the value YOU bring to them and their businesses. Your JV partner(s) should send out the announcements as follows:

1. Announcement #1 – 4 weeks prior to training
2. Announcement #2 – 2 weeks prior to training
3. Announcement #3 – 1 week prior to training
4. Announcement #4 – 48 hours prior to training

Use the following as an example of the e-mail training announcement to be sent by your JV partner:

****

Subject: Unlock $100,000 Potential for Your Business

Samantha Smith, a leading marketing strategist, will be doing some LIVE TRAINING, where he/she will share how to unlock a $100,000 revenue opportunity for your business.

Samantha will share her eight easy-to-implement profit generation strategies that can EASILY add more than $100,000 to ANY small business's bottom line.

There are no gimmicks. The eight strategies that Samantha will share with you are fundamental to all businesses, but for some reason, no one is using them.

Would an additional $100,000 this year, and next year, and EVERY year after that help you out financially???

This training is for ANY small business owner who wants to see an IMMEDIATE increase in both their revenue and profits.

Please join Samantha for this revenue optimization opportunity.

Training Date:

Training Time:

Venue:

Register online at www.samanthasmithtraining.com

P.S. There will be NO fluff, and NO generic content presented. Everything offered in this presentation has but ONE GOAL – to make you more money immediately!

****

Once the JV partner of your choice has sent the invites to their database, and you have local business owners registered for your training session, please be sure to invite your JV business partner to your training event as a Guest Speaker or Sponsor, to allow them an opportunity to do their pitch about their services for the first ten minutes of the event.

Strategy #2: Start Conducting Marketing

Bootcamp Sessions Regularly

Having offline training events is the best-kept lead generation secret for business coaches. While many business coaches are moving their lead generation strategies online by conducting Webinars, posting to Facebook groups, etc. offline events by far are the most cost-effective and efficient ways to generate leads that you desperately need. Don't get me wrong: I'm not against digital marketing lead generation strategies for business coaches, but if you want to get your leads fast for a nominal investment, go offline. Do those events often, and most importantly, consistently.

For a successful Bootcamp, do this:

✓ **Have a good Bootcamp Agenda:** The Agenda must be well-thought-out. The agenda items should result in an authentic learning experience for the business owners. Examples of agenda items are as follows:

- *Seven Proven Marketing Strategies to Help You Generate Cash Right Away*
- *Never Pay for Advertising Again*

- *How to Raise Your Prices Without Losing a Single Customer.*

Here is the sample agenda for your Bootcamp:

Agenda: ***Seven Proven Marketing Strategies to Help You Generate Cash Right Away***

Time	Activity
7:15am	Doors Open/Breakfast/Coffee setup/Mingling
7:15-7:30am	Participants Sign in/Breakfast/Coffee/Mingling
7:30 -7:45 am	Introductions (60 seconds per participant: Name, type of business, pain points)
7:45-9:00 am	Presentation
9:00 -9:15 am	Questions/Close/Surveys completed/Collect Participants' business cards

You can plan your session in such a way that you hit several topics at a time, or you can pick just one problem and expand on it during the time you set aside for training. Having an agenda that fulfills your customer's needs is 90 percent of your training success. What is the other 10 percent? Well-planned logistics! To have a successful event, make sure you:

✓ **Decide on the date and time of your training**: I recommend Tuesday between 7:30-9:30 am. Business owners are extremely busy people wearing many hats. Catching them before 10 am is critical. Some of my fellow business coaches are very successful in running their Bootcamps during the lunch hour time. I suggest that you try both to see what works best for you and the business owners. It is important that you keep your event under two hours. If it runs longer, you may lose your attendees' attention and, in fact, most of them as they would be headed back to their offices to take care of their businesses.

✓ **Choose a good venue**. By *"good"* venue, I mean affordable, accessible, comfortable, and Audio-Visual (AV) equipped. What works best? Think about a room at the local Chapter of the Business Network International (BNI) office, Chamber of Commerce (you will find it surprisingly affordable), a local business incubator, office sharing facilities, senior living communities, or a hotel. Renting a meeting room at the local hotel might be surprisingly inexpensive. I recommend that you ask for a classroom set up to be arranged by your conference room provider. The room that you'll need for your training should accommodate up to 20 people.

EXPERT TIP: **Should you decide to rent a conference room from a hotel, ask them about their catering fee (coffee, refreshments, or continental breakfast). It is not uncommon for most of the hotels to include catering for a nominal fee into a room rental. For example, the room rental alone can be $70/ hour with a two-hour minimum. With catering, it might be only $90 with a two-hour minimum (these prices may vary depending on the event geographical location). There is always room for negotiation. Remember, the hotel wants your business. If you let them know that you are going to run those trainings on a regular basis (once monthly or bi-monthly), they will most likely give you the best deal. Just ask for it.**

✓ **Have your Web designer build an eye-catching Bootcamp registration page**: The registration page will have all your Bootcamp details such as date, time, whether breakfast or lunch are provided, event agenda, and expected outcomes.

Example of the text for the registration page:

****

Everything You Know About Generating Leads, Closing Sales and Making Money With Your Small Business Is WRONG!

All we need is just 90-minute of your time to spend with a group of successful local [name of your city] business owners and learning new ways to double or triple your leads. We will show you how using the seven proven, simple, actionable business growth strategies.

Breakfast is on us! To reserve your seat, register **HERE.**

****

- ✓ **Send Eye-Catching E-mail Invites with a link to your event registration page:**

  - Announcement #1 – 4 weeks prior to training
  - Announcement #2 – 2 weeks prior to training
  - Announcement #3 – 1 week prior to training
  - Announcement #4 – 48 hours prior to training

NOTE: Feel free to customize or reuse the training announcement in its entirety provided earlier in this book.

If you are just starting out and don't have enough customers in your database, work with your JV partner(s) to send e-mail announcements on your behalf. Other options include:

- Using the Event Brite (https://www.eventbrite.com/) platform
- Creating an event on Facebook and promoting it to the local businesses
- Posting your event on the local Chamber of Commerce calendar

- Posting your event on the calendar of events hosted by the local newspaper (online and in print)

- Advertising your event on the local radio station

- Promoting your event to the local office share places and business incubators. In exchange, offer to provide a FREE consultation to a few tenants.

- Promoting your event through local business networking groups. In exchange, offer to pay for the initial coaching session for 2-3 networking group members.

✓ **Secure Audio Visual (AV) devices**: You must make arrangements for a microphone, clicker, laptop, projector, and cords. Have your PowerPoint presentation ready and tested at least a week before the event.

✓ **Secure Supplies**: A week before the session, secure supplies like a flip chart, whiteboard, registration desk, wastebasket, pads, pens, background music, candy and water stations, name tags, markers, sign-in sheet, sticky notes, at least 30 copies of the agenda, your business cards, and books.

✓ **Secure Refreshments**: It is your choice if you want to offer a full hot breakfast, continental breakfast, or just light refreshments that would include coffee, water, and candy. It all depends on the budget you have. Light refreshments can help you retain the invitees in the room longer since the attention span of an average person is about 20 minutes. Lack of refreshments may cause your participants to start leaving the room to get their own. I'd advise including at least coffee and a snack during the training.

✓ **Plan out a Good Closing**: Before you end your session, simply ask the participants, *"Do you want my help?"* Make sure you offer your advice and contact information (phone, e-mail, Website). Offer to pay for their first coaching session.

✓ **Have the Participants Complete a Survey**: At the end of the session, ask your attendees to evaluate your Bootcamp by asking them a few simple questions. For example:

- On a scale of 0 to 5 where the 5 is *"Outstanding,"* how would you rate today's session?

- What was your key takeaway from today's session?
- What areas of the Bootcamps do we need to improve to make it more beneficial to you?
- Please provide a referral business, so they benefit from this session as well.*

The latter is important because once you have referrals, this can help you generate additional leads at no cost to you.

✓ **Have a Sign-in Sheet:** Make sure all participants sign in and provide their contact info. Give them assurances that you will not be spamming them.

✓ **Be sure to Collect Participants' Business Cards:** This is one of the first and the easiest step to start building your customer database. As a courtesy and part of business etiquette, be sure to offer yours as well.

✓ **Follow up**: You have invested time and money into your Bootcamp Training. It is essential that you follow up with your warm leads with a call or e-mail to schedule an appointment. Make sure you follow up within 24 hours after the Bootcamp Training. Participants' business cards that you have collected during the Bootcamp event will turn out to be helpful for this purpose.

Also, after the end of the session, you can hand out brochures for future meetings. This will generate interest. After this session ends, you can offer a sign up for your paid coaching service packages. Some of the participants will likely sign up immediately! So, stay ready with sign-up forms.

Strategy #3: Attend Local Business Networking Events

So, you have just started your business, and you are looking to make some valuable connections with other businesses that might need your services. There is no better way to achieve this than by attending local business networking events.

Business networking can help you reach more clients and maybe even find a JV Partner. It can also help you boost your profits and expand your business. That's because, during these events, you are most likely to meet people who have been on the same path as you are right now and get some valuable advice from them.

Here are some of the best business networking groups

that you should join:

- BNI – Business Networking International
- Mastermind Groups
- LeTip
- Meetup
- Alignable
- Women In Business Networking
- CVB
- Chamber of Commerce
- Kiwanis
- Rotary Club International
- Optimists
- 1Million Cups (https://www.1millioncups.com/)

Online business networking groups:

- YEC - Young Entrepreneurs' Council (yec.co)
- Small Giants Virtual Peer Groups (content.smallgiants.org)

- YPO – Young Presidents' Organization (ypo.org)
- StartupNation (community.startupnation.com)
- Ryze (www.ryze.com)
- Opportunity

Strategy #4: Become a Member of the Local Chamber of Commerce

Of all the groups previously listed, I would most recommend joining the Chamber of Commerce for the massive exposure to local business owners through the Chamber-hosted networking events. The Chamber of Commerce hosts conferences, training, workshops, happy hour events, ribbon-cutting ceremonies, and *"business after-hours"* events. It also releases publications and business directories.

The Chamber of Commerce is always looking for ways to educate its members with regard to innovative business growth strategies. You, as a business coach, become an invaluable resource for the Chamber in helping the Chamber to support their mission of HELPING LOCAL BUSINESSES GROW. It is a win-win situation.

Start by networking with other Chamber members just to get your feet wet. Get the vibe of the Chamber members, talk to them, listen to their needs, feel their pain points, get some insights into their business, and issues they are dealing with. When introducing yourself, make sure you introduce yourself not as a business coach but rather as a person who *"helps businesses grow."* Approach the Chamber Training Point of Contact with an offer of free training for the members. Become their *"go-to"* person for any business growth and strategic marketing needs. If such a person already exists, find out their name and try to team up with them for better efficiency.

Offer no-cost *"limited time only"* one-on-one business coaching sessions to the Chamber members. It can be one or two sessions. At the end of the last session, ask them if they further need your help. If they do, offer them one of the packages that best suit their needs.

Strategy #5: Use Local Business Listings

Listing your business in local business directories is another excellent way to expose your services to your potential clients. You can list your business in platforms such as Google Places, Yellow pages, Yelp (https://www.yelp.com/), and many other similar platforms.

Be aware that listing your business on any business listings requires a fee. Make the best pick based on your budget. Before investing in any such platform, calculate your Return on Investment (ROI).

Strategy #6: Become a Member on Alignable

Alignable (https://www.alignable.com/) is a great online platform that I recommend every business owner join. It is made to offer helpful advice, support, and insights to all its members. The main goal of this platform is to create a network of like-minded people that help each other regarding their businesses. You can use this platform to build credibility for your business and generate referrals.

Once you become a member of Alignable, you can start "talking" to business owners. You can survey their needs and what kind of challenges they are experiencing. Once you have connected with a business owner, invite them for a cup of coffee to continue the conversation. You may need several meetings with a business owner before you can offer your services. However, it is not uncommon for a business owner to request your help right away.

Strategy #7: Hold Seminars/Webinars or Give Workshops

Conducting live events like seminars, webinars, or workshops on lead-generation strategies always draws business owners' attention. It is a great way to bring value to the community, help business owners improve their bottom line, and promote your services.

Strategy #8: Read the Ads in Industry Publications, Journals, or Websites

This would be an excellent start to get your first clients since those portals target their advertising to the same group of people that you are targeting. Focus on ads written by small businesses and follow up with them to offer help generating more leads.

Strategy #9: Ask Local Radio Stations to Promote Your Bootcamp, Presentation, or Live Event

A radio announcement has the potential to reach your audience. People listen to podcasts, and radio shows to stay updated with the latest news on the go. Send an announcement of your presentation or event to a local radio station to grab your audience's attention.

Strategy #10: Contact a Local Newspaper

Contact your local newspaper. Offer a free coaching session on how to generate more leads for their circulation. In exchange, ask them to publish an article about you highlighting your knowledge and expertise.

Whichever marketing strategy you choose to start with, be sure to show the customer the value you bring. Stating the value in your marketing messages is critically important for establishing yourself as an expert business coach and showcasing your ability to help business owners grow and generate more revenue. This is the ultimate goal of the business coaching profession. The next section should provide you with key strategies to do this.

One of the quick, inexpensive, and most importantly, effective ways to generate leads is to conduct free "Lunch-n-Learn" events for local business

networking groups, business incubators, or office sharing facilities. Pick a topic that your attendees would benefit from and go over your strategies to help solve business owners' headaches. Make sure you plan out and conduct those events on a regular basis. When conducting your "Lunch-n-Learn" events, it is important that you make them as personable and customized to the business owners' needs as much as possible. Set aside enough time for questions and answers. Make it truly a Lunch and Learn event for the attendees.

Chapter Summary

Generating leads offline remains by far the best-kept secret in Business Coaching. Nothing is more beneficial for business owners than a well-planned, well-executed, high-value LOCAL event conducted by a LOCAL Marketing Guru who offers them actionable strategies to scale their business. Institute and start conducting live events on a regular basis. It is very important that the topics you are offering bring value to your attendees. Just enter the conversation that is taking place in their heads and help them get rid of their pain points by addressing them during your live events.

Coaching Assignment #5:

Identify business networking events in your area and go ahead and join some of them. Start attending those to get an idea of the local business pain points. Start offering your help and solutions, as necessary.

Chapter 6
Use These Long-Term Strategies to Help Scale Your Coaching Business

EXPERT TIP **It is important that you NOT use ALL the strategies outlined in this chapter at the same time. Pick a few that you feel most comfortable with and put them to work.**

You may be the best business coach out there, but that does not guarantee you success. Many factors come together to build a successful business. One of them is a marketing strategy that gives your business a competitive edge!

This chapter focuses on the coaches-tested and approved strategies to help you grow your business long term. We will discuss each strategy in this chapter in detail.

Create a Website

A Website represents the identity of any business online. It offers prospective clients a convenient way to access the company and its services. It gives a face to the business, and it is, in many cases, the reason for a business that is going great. Create a Website for your business coaching services so people can identify you among the many other business coaches. When populating your Website with content, make sure you have a message of what value you provide to your ideal customer. Make sure to provide metrics of what you are capable of delivering to your customers such as a timeframe (*"Give me 30 days, and I'll show you how to generate $20,000 in additional revenue"*), expected results (*"I will show you how to double your revenue in six months"*), etc.

Perform Search Engine Optimization (SEO)

Having a Website is great, but if your potential customers can't see or find it, that's useless no matter how much valuable content you are going to put on it. That's why your site will need Search Engine Optimization (SEO) to help you put your Website in front of potential customers. I gathered some tips and tricks for you on the best ways to do the SEO for your site, so you have more leads and inquiries about your services.

Create Your Business Landing Page

When it comes to Website vs. landing page, the significant difference between these two is that a Website serves as your entire online first impression. The landing page, on the other hand, can be considered as a greeting page for new customers. In some instances, the Website might be more effective than a landing page and vice versa.

Before your clients find your Website, they discover your landing page. A landing page is focused only on one message, and that pertains to converting the visitor of your Website into a buyer. A landing page doesn't have any links, so the visitor has no distractions, and they only concentrate on the message your page is giving.

A landing page has the following characteristics:

- It is a one-pager.
- It has only one purpose. (Conversion of prospects)
- It has a clear Call-To-Action.

- You can identify a landing page with many different names:

Sign-up landing page, click-through landing page, and reference landing page. It has several benefits, including but not limited to, the following:

Building Your E-mail List

A landing page is a quick way to build it. You can display your landing page as a sign-up form to your prospects. When they sign up to receive your e-mails, promotions, or notifications, they give you their e-mail address in the signup form. In this way, your e-mail lists build up automatically.

Enticing Prospects to Stay Connected with You

You can add a contest on your landing page so you can entice your prospects to participate. In this way, they stay connected with you in the hopes of winning a prize. Also, when they win, you can offer them one of your business/marketing coaching sessions for free. You will be able to advertise your services in this way. Moreover, you will be able to get sign-ups for your future paid sessions.

Selling Directly to Your Prospects

You can sell your sessions directly to your prospects through your landing page.

Building Relationships with the Prospects

A landing page helps your prospects stay in touch with you since the inception of your business leads them to your Website and offers them the option to choose for your services straight away. It helps you in building a relationship with your customers that lasts a lifetime.

Perform Direct Mail Marketing Campaigns

Direct mail marketing allows you to send details about your business coaching products to your clients. According to a report of the Direct Marketing Association (DMA) published in 2003, the average response rate to direct mails was 5.1 percent in 2017.

This is the highest response rate ever reported by the DMA. This report shows that direct mail works. It is the most effective tool to grab the attention of consumers, which not only makes them respond but also compels them to take action. Here are some tips you can use for boosting your business coaching practice through direct mail marketing.

1. **Understand your target audience.** The most critical part of using direct mail marketing is to understand your target audience. Knowing about their concerns and requirements is the key factor here. Knowing about your client's priorities and approaches will help you a great deal. So, when buying a database for your direct marketing campaign, make sure you buy the correct target audience data, which for a business coach would be small and medium-sized business owners.

2. **Focus on the Offer.** Your ultimate goal is to help your customers generate more cash than ever before. So, your offer that you are going to send via direct mail must focus on the value that you will bring to your customer. **BIG, BOLD VALUE.** Decide whether it is going to be just one offer, two, or even three offers that you are going to send them via direct mail. For example:

- *Want to know why everything you know about marketing ...is wrong?*
- *Want to make $50,000 in **ADDITIONAL** revenue*

IN ONLY 30 DAYS?

- *I can help you generate all the leads you can handle*

- *Do you want to learn how NOT TO SPEND ANY MONEY ON ADVERTISING and STILL GROW your business?*

- *Call me at 555-555-55-55 to learn how to double your current profits within just 90 days.*

3. **Timing is everything.** Just like e-mail, timing plays a significant role when it comes to getting a response from your clients using direct mail. I recommend that you halt your direct marketing campaigns during the November-December timeframe and don't resume until mid-January.

Consistency

When your mails display a similar pattern to your clients, it builds consistency on your part, and they begin to trust you as an authentic business. You can add consistency by adding a general line or slogan that only you can use. You should even get a copyright for it to make sure you can use the same line in each of your mails. The paper you print the mails on should be your business letterhead, so people recognize your business and services at one glance.

Create Sales Videos

There's no denying the power of video when it comes to attracting customers and promoting any services. People don't have time to read, research, and reach out to you if they need some sort of help. In this case, a video is a great tool to reach people and to make your services known to them. Video is known as rich media content, and it can boost customer engagement, increase the time spent on a site, and help convert prospects into paying customers. Used cleverly and with a purpose, a video can transform your Website into a dynamic interactive site that will attract repeat visits. Most video services allow their users to discover your videos via their Websites and apps. You can usually embed videos on your Website - and in other locations, such as your tweets, Facebook pages, and Instagram posts.

Following are some crucial points to bear in mind while making a sales video to promote business/marketing coaching:

1. Create Useful Content. Your customers have questions. They want to understand better how to use your business/marketing coaching services. By creating a series of informational videos, you can provide value to your customers; It works as a form of customer service. You can also answer some of the frequently asked questions through videos. In this way, your customer service help will not be overcrowded.

2. Create a Case Study and "Dissect" it in the video explaining what mistakes the small business owner makes and what's the best way to handle it. The video doesn't have to be long. Up to five minutes max. The goal of the video is to present meaningful content by providing the info/facts that the small business owner doesn't know, thus entice the business owner, who is a potential customer to call up the business coach, a.k.a. YOU to request their services. For example, *"How to Boost Your Sales Without Spending a Dime on Advertising."*

3. Be an Expert. Make your audience feel that you are the one who can help them move forward and overcome their challenges growing their business. Create a series of videos in which you share your expertise. Once you create the videos, share them across all your social media channels and make them available on your website.

4. Use Live Streaming. Social media is currently riding the video wave, with free tools such as Google Hangouts (https://hangouts.google.com/) and new tools like Periscope (https://www.pscp.tv/). These services are creating raving fans of live streaming. It's still in the early days for these tools, so be an early adopter and establish yourself as a live streaming professional. You can stay available for your clientele anywhere and anytime through live streaming. There is no way they will miss even a single session of yours with these tools.

5. Apply Continuity. Make a series of videos on a specific topic so that your audience understands your concept well and release them consistently. Answer questions asked by various customers on your Website.

6. Have a Personal Touch. Invite customers to your Website; introduce your services to them. It helps you to develop relationships with your customers. This will help them in deciding whether they want your help or not.

7. Have a Helping Attitude. Always maintain a helping attitude towards your clients. Never focus on sales in your video because your clients might think that your priority is just to sell your services. This will discourage them from buying your services.

8. Use Client Testimonials. Many coaches use written testimonials on their Websites. However, you can create more interest and authenticity if you interview small business owners or invite customers to upload their videos using your services.

To promote your sales videos, use these Websites:

- https://www.youtube.com/
- http://www.dailymotion.com/pk
- https://vimeo.com

Use Facebook

A business coach needs a platform to reach out to maximum clients. Along with various other platforms to promote business coaching, Facebook is one of the quickest and the most reliable means. Remember, though, most business owners don't spend much time on Facebook simply because they are too busy growing their business.

How to Best Use Facebook to Promote Your Coaching Services?

Following are the five most powerful and useful tips to promote your business coaching services:

1. Use Facebook Ads: Facebook Ads are one of the best tools to promote your coaching services. There are multiple options available to use Facebook advertisements. You have complete flexibility when choosing budget, details, and the content of your own choice. Another great benefit of Facebook ads is that you can retarget your old clients, fans, and Website visitors. This way, you can expose your ads to people who have already shown interest in your business and your offers.

2. Create a Facebook Business Page: Creating your own Facebook business coaching page is another tool that can help you promote your services. Having your own Facebook business page will make it easier for you to interact with your customers or visitors. It will attract more and more visitors to subscribe to your services.

3. Integrate a Bot with your FB Business Page: When it comes to bots, one of the best apps that you can find on the market is ManyChat (https://manychat.com).

ManyChat is the number one bot platform on Facebook Messenger for support, marketing, and e-commerce. This app has 80 percent open rates and 25 percent CTR (Click-Through-Rate). Many studies have predicted that Messenger is the future of digital marketing, and this fact is pretty visible if you explore options on social media. Many customers prefer sending messages to their favorite brands instead of calling them because it is much more convenient. ManyChat helps promote your products/services, takes payments from your clients, and qualifies leads through Facebook Messenger. All of these qualities of the app are useful for promoting your business coaching services. Therefore, ManyChat is the one for you[1].

Chatbots respond to customers quickly, and they are only improving as time passes.

Tools to be Used to Promote Your Business Coaching via Facebook:

- https://www.facebook.com/business/
- https://www.facebook.com/business/products/ads can be used to create ads for your services.

---

[1] Meet Messenger Marketing: https://manychat.com/

- https://www.facebook.com/business/products/ads/ad-targeting can be used to target the audience of your interest. Clients who are looking for your services can be easily targeted.
- https://www.facebook.com/business/products/pages can be used to create your business page.
- https://coschedule.com/headline-analyzer. It can be used to make readers see your posts.
- https://sumo.com/app/share. This tool makes it stupid-easy for your visitors to share your content with their friends, family, and others with built-in social media buttons for your site. The more people share your site and content, the more traffic you can get for your Website.
- https://www.postplanner.com. It makes social media marketing simple for small business owners by providing a suite of tools to engage followers. It features tools for cover photos, contests, custom tabs, scheduled posts, Facebook ads, and more.
- https://www.shortstack.com. ShortStack is a self-service platform that helps in building engaging

social media campaigns for you. The platform features more than 30 widgets, 30 themes, and 90 templates, all of which you can use to build contests and sweepstakes, special offers, landing pages, custom forms, and more.

Use E-mail Marketing

E-mail marketing is a tool to leverage the power of e-mail to reach out to your target clients and become able to promote your coaching services. It is one of the best ways to keep in contact with your customers and keep them updated with all of your services and developments. E-mail marketing is one of the easiest and inexpensive ways of staying in touch with your customers.

How to Use E-mail Marketing for Promotion?

The idea behind e-mail marketing is that you must maintain a list of clients, customers, and subscribers who are interested in hearing something about your services. You manage your e-mail list of customer base using one of the Customer Relationship Management (CRM) tools.

Customer Relationship Management (CRM)

CRM is a system for managing interactions and relationships of an organization with potential customers. The main goal of a CRM system is to help companies in staying connected with customers and improve the profitability of the business.

CRM software stores all necessary customer information such as e-mail addresses, phone numbers, social media profile links, Website addresses, if any, and other useful information that you can use to get in touch with your prospects or clients. It automatically extracts additional information as well, such as new details about the company's activity. It records details such as the client's personal preferences on communications.

The following are some of the best CRM systems you can find in the market today:

- SalesForce Sales Cloud (https://www.salesforce.com/products/sales-cloud/overview/)

- HubSpot CRM (https://www.hubspot.com/products/crm)

- Freshsales CRM (https://www.freshworks.com/freshsales-crm/)
- Mail Chimp CRM (https://mailchimp.com/features/crm/)
- Zoho (https://www.zoho.com/crm/)
- AWeber CRM (https://www.aweber.com/integrations/crm/index.htm)
- Keap CRM (https://keap.com/)
- PipeDrive (https://www.pipedrive.com/en-gb)
- Insightly (https://www.insightly.com/)
- Nimble CRM (https://www.nimble.com/)
- Spiro CRM (https://spiro.ai/)

The CRM tool of your choice enables you to send out e-mails to your database bearing news of services that they feel are beneficial and useful for them. It would help if you adopted the following strategies to promote your coaching services using e-mail marketing.

    a. **Generate Valuable Content**. To start with e-mail marketing for your services, you must have valuable content, which keeps your audience engaged. You must have content that benefits your customers.

b. **Create and Maintain Your Customer E-mail List.** You must have an e-mail list with maximum possible contacts. You can maintain an e-mail list by importing your existing customers into your CRM tool.

c. **Send out Subscriber E-mails on a Regular Basis (Drip Campaign).**

A drip campaign is a method that is used in direct marketing to capture prospects. This campaign comprises of sending marketing information to potential customers over a repeatedly longer period to nurture the leads through the marketing funnel.

Drip campaigns are mostly executed through e-mail marketing. In this way, pre-written e-mail content is automatically sent to the contact over a decided period of time to keep them engaged.

There are many tools available in the market that can automate dripping e-mails such as marketing automation from Eloqua, Hubspot, Marketo, Pardot, and others.

The following are some of the benefits of drip campaigns:

Create Higher Engagement

Drip campaigns ensure that e-mails are sent to prospects who are interested in your products and services. They are more effective than the usual e-mail campaigns.

Save Time and Effort

Drip campaigns ensure the automated funnel movement. In this way, you can save a lot of time and effort that you can utilize in focusing on other tasks.

Prospects Aren't Annoyed

Drip campaigns only send e-mails when customers want to see them. In this way, they are more welcoming to the e-mails. Usual e-mail campaigns can be very annoying sometimes and may irritate customers.

Subscriber e-mails are part of the drip campaign. You must send subscriber e-mails consistently. Pick the frequency and stick with it. I recommend at least twice a month. To help pique your subscriber base interest, choose a topic, and break its content for several e-mailings. For example, *"The Top Five Lead Generation Strategies for Your Business;"* Subsequently, you will need to send five e-mails outlining one strategy per e-mail. Always end your e-mail with a closing statement that would hold your subscribers' interest until the next e-mail.

Tools to Use for Successful E-mail Marketing:
- https://www.ianbrodie.com
- https://www.formget.com/
- http://www.whenigrowupcoach.com/oneonone/
- https://www.constantcontact.com/home-page
- https://www.drip.com
- https://convertkit.com
- https://www.getresponse.com
- https://mailchimp.com
- https://www.activecampaign.com

Use Click Funnels

Click Funnels (https://www.clickfunnels.com/) offers the service of processing payments digitally and integrates with Stripe, Recurly, NMI, and more. Unlike competitor products, which allow you to create single standalone pages, Click Funnels is all about building different types of marketing funnels. A funnel is a series of pages your visitors go through to reach a particular goal. The first thing you have to know to get the most out of Click Funnels is what you're going to use the system for. Click Funnels is a self-contained service. That means that when you subscribe to Click Funnels, you don't need to have an autoresponder. However, if you already have an autoresponder that works well for you, Click Funnels can integrate with them and be a backup in case your autoresponder loses data.

Use Click Funnels to promote and grow your business as follows:

- **Thank People:** Create a Thank You page, which is an excellent gesture for your clients who will be motivated to take the next step, which is the Call to Action. It will help in your future conversation with your clients. For example, you can tell people to check their inbox for sign-up confirmation, invite them to set an intention for your work together, and share what they're about to do with you on social media! It's also a great way to direct them to join your Facebook group and more.

- **Upgrade Content:** You can add a Call to Action button. It is usually found at the bottom of a blog post designed to direct readers to extra-high-value content. It's a great way to share more of your whip-smart knowledge with your peers and build your e-mail subscriber list at the same time. Click Funnels lets you add an opt-in box to any page you'd like, including for example, right in the middle or end of your blog post – which makes it beyond easy to promote your content upgrade just when your reader is feeling super excited to get their hands on the exclusive extra content you're offering.

- **Host Paid Content:** If you ever share info sheets, templates, screencast tutorials, video training or any other kind of content with only your paid clients, you can use Click Funnels to create and host all of that so that you can share it exclusively via a secret URL with clients.

- **Launch a Package:** Click Funnels makes it super easy to build multi-step sales funnels where you can share lots of great content to help you improve your subscriber list, amplify your standing as an expert, and promote your signature package.

- **Host a Replay:** You can set up a special broadcast room right there in the platform that you can integrate with your preferred Webinar service. You can use Click Funnels to customize your Webinar *"room"* with your visual branding, vibe, and key messages and calls to action.

- **Add a Pop-Up to Your Website:** Click Funnels ClickPops feature makes it utterly easy to create customized pop-ups and set the timeframe for when they appear so that they can be as *"in your face"* or unobtrusive as you like.

- **Integrate with Facebook:** Click Funnels has a unique plug-in tool that makes it easy to add a tab to your Facebook Business page that links directly to your opt-in, sales page, or registration landing page.

Additional Resources to Help You Grow Your Business Using Click Funnels

- https://blog.clickfunnels.com
- https://www.groovymarketing.biz/blog/2016/11/21/clickfunnels-pricing-etison-suite

Use Blogs

A blog is a representation of who you are and what your thoughts are on the Web. Promoting your business services includes the ability to produce and distribute quality content to all your clients promptly. Many platforms offer blogging capability. However, WordPress (https://wordpress.com/) stands out due to its simplicity and versatility when it comes to blogging capability.

Benefits of using a blog to promote your business services include but not limited to:

a. **Cost-effectiveness:** There are many blogging platforms where you can use blogs to promote your business coaching without paying too much Web domain expenses.

b. **Ease of Use:** Most blogging platforms provide you the flexibility of making your blogs.

c. **Helps Attract Customers:** Offering useful content, thoughts, ideas, and updates give you a great opportunity to attract maximum clients to look for your services.

d. **Helps Expand Your Services:** The nature of blogs is such that it can generate online conversations and discussions, which increases the chances of people learning about your coaching services.

e. **Provides Valuable Feedback:** Blog is a platform, which brings in ideas, observations, and feedback to your services. If you get positive feedback, it will boost your confidence; if you get some negative feedback, it provides you an opportunity to resolve their complaints. By doing this, you will develop the trust of your clients, and they will take a step forward to seek your coaching services.

f. **Boosts SEO:** By using blogs to promote your coaching services, you will provide Google and other search engines new content and ideas. Your visibility to search engine results will increase, and you will reach more clients by continuous blogging.

g. **Helps Develop Relationships:** Blogs provide you with an opportunity to develop strong relations with your clients. You can invite visitors to comment on a particular subject or thought.

h. **Allows Sharing Opportunity:** With blogs, you can share your thoughts and opinions on the Web with all of your customers.

There are six ways to use your blogs for promoting your coaching services:

a. **Create an Attractive Outline Platform**: You will need to create an attractive outline platform by putting some effort into it so that it is appealing for your visitors and audiences. Make sure that the images you are using in your content are attractive and relate to your theme.

b. **Create Valuable Content**: Make sure that your content revolves around the pain points that your customers are having. When developing high-value content, enter the conversation taking place in the heads of your customers and come up with the solutions.

c. **Create a Series of Interviews:** Clients or audiences love talking about themselves, their goals, and their problems. Create a series of interviews on your blog to develop your relationships further offline.

d. **Use Call-to-Action:** You must include Call to Action at the end of your blogs so that your audience takes action after reading your blog. The call to action may consist of words like Register, Subscribe, Share, or Questions.

e. **Continue Building Your E-Mail List:** Use your blogs to continue building the e-mail list that you will use to market your offerings.

f. **Use Social Media:** Tag other people and organizations in your content to extend your reach to clients. Create audience-focused and professional content. Make use of media like Facebook, Twitter, etc. to increase your traffic of clients. Blogs will work perfectly well when used in conjunction with other marketing tools like Facebook and Twitter.

Here are some tips on promoting your blog.

After creating and integrating your blog to promote business coaching with your Website, you need to promote it using different social media tools like Twitter, Tumblr (https://www.tumblr.com/), LinkedIn, and Facebook. When clients visit your blog and start a conversation with you, you can also ask them to share it with other people.

Assign Responsibly

Sometimes, you just don't have the time to manage your blog yourself. Therefore, you must assign this responsibility to someone who can keep your blog updated by adding the progress of your business on it. As a business/marketing coach, you don't have to be a great writer, so it is not necessary that you will be able to produce quality blogs. To resolve this issue, you can hire help from outside. Any experienced blogger would love to market your coaching services for the right incentive. Your potential and existing clients would like to know more about the achievements of your business.

Attract Subscribers

Blogs automatically motivate readers to subscribe via

Really Simple Syndication (RSS), which tells them about an update on your blog. Clients or visitors also prefer receiving notifications via e-mail. This will attract a large number of clients to subscribe to your blog and eventually seek your coaching services.

Comment on Other Blogs

If you comment on other people's blogs and post backlinks of your Website, it provides a wonderful opportunity for you to attract clients or visitors from other blogs to your blog. It increases your visibility and traffic to your coaching services.

Marketing of your business coaching through blog posts is a powerful tool today. It is one of the easiest and most effective ways to reach maximum clients with your services at a low cost and reasonably quickly. It is hardly a difficult task to maximize the visibility of your business. You just have to follow basic guidelines using the tool of blog marketing, and you will see your customer base multiply.

These are the tools/to be used to promote your blog.

- https://www.semrush.com
- https://www.9sites.net/

- http://www.bloggernity.com/
- http://blogswirl.com
- http://ezinearticles.com/
- http://www.articlebiz.com/
- http://www.a1articles.com/
- http://www.articlegeek.com/
- http://www.sooperarticles.com/

Use Pay-Per-Click (PPC) Ads

PPC is a method of digital marketing in which advertisers pay a certain fee whenever their ad is clicked. It is a way of buying visits to your site rather than working to *"earn"* the visits.

Search engine Websites, especially Google, is the most visited Website in the world. This is why advertising on search results holds so much importance. If executed properly, PPC can be quite beneficial for you. For example, let's say you are paying $1 per click. However, that click eventually results in a $997 sale.

Therefore, you end up with a hefty profit. A good PPC campaign requires a lot of hard work and research before it becomes beneficial for you. Most importantly, you need to select the right keywords and then organize them in the right way to make PPC work. Other than that, you also need to ensure that ads are of the highest quality and relevant. Search engines give preference to high-quality ads[2].

Here is a myth that PPC is way too expensive to use it for promotions. The reason behind that is that people focus way too much on making sales of their services in their promotional advertisement and do not focus on attracting customers. This is the biggest mistake you can make while attempting to use pay per click advertisement. If you do not take care of this aspect, it may affect your advertising campaign terribly.

Making Sale vs. Acquiring Customers

Many business coaches get confused while using pay per click advertising to promote their services. The reason

---

[2]WordStream (2019). What is PPC? Learn the Basics of Pay-Per-Click (PPC) Marketing. Retrieved from: https://www.wordstream.com/ppc

is that they do not know the difference between selling and acquiring new clients. Aim to convince people to approach your time and again rather than just offering your services to them once. It will benefit you long-term.

How to Use PPC for Promoting Coaching Services?

Pay per click advertisement is an auction where different people bid against a particular keyword to show up on a top spot in a search engine. The purpose of trying to get the top ranking in any search engine is to get maximum clients. When your Website URL ranks on top of the search engine, your Website will be the first link that a potential client will click on. It will increase your chances of retaining that client lead.

Converting Visitors into Paying Clients

After spending money and creating your PPC advertisement, create a goal to convert all visitors into paying customers. Follow these strategies to convert visitors into paying customers. **Identify Keywords**. You must identify the keywords which your target clients will enter into any search engine when they go looking for coaching services.

1. Structure Your PPC Advertisement Right. People go online for a reason. They need to find precise answers to their problems. Therefore, develop a problem-solving structure for your campaign.

2. Create Relevant Information. To maximize your traffic, make sure the information you are sharing is relevant to what the potential customers are looking for.

3. Link your PPC Ad to Your Landing Page. As a business coach, you have to make sure that you have a high converting landing page. Your PPC ads lead customers to your top converting landing page. A landing page is designed only for one reason – capture leads. So, when customers land on your landing page since it has no navigation, they have no choice other than pick up the phone straight away and call you to seek your services. Eventually, a high converting landing page can triple the number of calls, which one can expect.

4. Make it Easy for Customers. Getting clicks on your PPC ad is not enough to grow your coaching business. The important thing here is to make your visitors feel easy in taking the next step. Do not ask for too much in your first interaction.

5. Track Conversions. Always keep track of the visitors who convert to potential buyers.

6. Maintain a Good Writing Style. PPC ads require that your writing is short, meaningful, and catchy. Visitors click your ads and go away. Therefore, you must include only those words that are meaningful to visitors and encourage them to take the next step. For example, *"Help with doubling or tripling your leads," I help businesses thrive," "Don't spend a cent on marketing or advertising. I'll show you how."*

7. Maintain a Mailing List. E-mail lists are a must for advertising your coaching services. Keep adding new leads to your existing e-mail list.

8. Promote Your PPC Advertisement. PPC campaigns can become very successful when you have set short-term goals for a particular Advertisement. Keep a deadline for your campaign, and when the deadline approaches, people do not want to miss an event. You will have more chances for visitors to sign-up right before the deadline.

9. **Recall Consumers**. Great use of PPC is to recall clients who had seen your Website before and had not asked for any of your coaching services. PPC advertisement is an excellent way to call such customers back to your domain.

Tools/Websites

- http://www.bidvertiser.com/
- http://www.revenuehits.com/
- http://www.infolinks.com/
- http://www.clicksor.com/
- http://www.media.net/
- http://www.media.net/
- http://www.affinity.com/
- https://www.google.com/adsense
- http://adhitz.com/

Buy Leads from Sales Genie

Sales Genie (https://www.salesgenie.com/) is a business and consumer database that you can buy leads from to promote your business coaching services. In Sales Genie, you can narrow your target audience by a ZIP Code, business size, industry, and more. Sales Genie is definitely one of the most effective ways to generate leads for your business.

Use Video Marketing

Video marketing is the most powerful tool that can be used to promote your coaching services. It is a cost-effective and targeted tool, which drives leads, traffic, and customers. The best thing about using video marketing is that you will be able to reach way more clients than you could reach by one –on – one coaching.

Here are some of the benefits of video marketing:

- It helps you connect with the audience and builds a relationship of trust.
- It is incredibly beneficent when it comes to SEO as it helps you build backlinks to your site.
- It boosts information retention. It is hard to

remember something that you read years ago, but you can easily recall an exciting video ad.

- Four times as many customers prefer watching a video instead of reading through a text description[3].

How to Create A Video?

You don't have to hire a videographer to make your video. That can be an option but not a compulsion. You can make your video yourself. Here are some essential guidelines before creating and publishing your video.

Making Titles

Note down ten questions that your clients ask you frequently. The next step is to see what those titles are. Formulate these can question into video titles. For example:

- *How to Reduce Marketing Costs?*

- *How to Generate Leads Fast without Breaking a Bank?*

- *How to Reduce your Operating Costs?*

---

[3] Stringfellow, A (2017). What is Video Marketing? Benefits, Challenges and Best Practices for a Successful Video Marketing Campaign. NG Data. Retrieved from: https://www.ngdata.com/what-is-video-marketing/

- *How to Convert Leads into Paying Customers?*
- *How to Skyrocket Profits and Dominate Markets?*

Research

Research the hot topics and make videos explaining how to resolve the issues. Be convincing and sincere in your desire to help your clients.

Define Your Role

Clients will never come to know about what you will get them unstuck from or how will you help them grow if you don't define exactly what you can do for them. For example, if you are a coach and help to boost the passion of your clients, then you have to tell your audience exactly that by being more specific.

Keep it Brief

While creating your video, make sure that you convey your idea in the shortest possible time. Otherwise, your audience may get bored. Clients need details about services quickly, and the majority of them prefer videos that are under three minutes in length.

Create a Video Tutorial

Video tutorials are easy to use and attract people who are looking for directions.

Platforms like YouTube, Facebook, Vimeo (https://vimeo.com), Periscope (https://www.periscope.tv), and Twitter are some of the best platforms to get your video viral. You can use many of these platforms for streaming live videos too. In this way, you will be saved from the hassle of recording and editing your videos. Live streaming videos have a much more positive effect than anything else.

Tools for Video Marketing

- https://www.mccabemarketing.ca/online-marketing-video-marketing
- https://www.youtube.com/
- http://www.dailymotion.com/pk
- https://www.worldcat.org/ For a keyword search
- https://books.google.com.pk/ For a keyword search

Write Articles and Publish them on E-zines or Any Other Online Platforms

Another very effective and low-cost way to market your business coaching service is to write articles about the value you bring to business owners. You can then get these articles published on some of the most popular E-zines, blogs, or any other type of news portal that you think would help you reach your potential audience. Being a published author provides you the credibility that is sought by most business owners when it comes to hiring a business/marketing coach business/marketing coach. Can't write? No worries. There are plenty of resources that would help you write your articles very inexpensively. Here are some resources that you can use:

List of freelance sources

- Flexjobs (www.flexjobs.com)
- Fiverr (www.fiverr.com)
- Upwork (www.upwork.com)
- CloudPeeps (www.cloudpeeps.com)

- Indeed (www.indeed.com)

- Freelancer (www.freelancer.com)

- Guru (www.guru.com)

- Craigslist (www.craigslist.org)

- Contena (www.contena.co)

- Journalism Jobs (www.journalismjobs.com)

- Due (www.due.com)

- Contently (contently.com)

- Behance (www.behance.net)

- Dribble (dribble.com)

E-zines and E-Articles Platforms

- Your Own Website's Blog

- https://ezinearticles.com/

- Buzzle.com

- Articlebase.com

- Goarticles.com

- Articlesfactory.com

- Findarticles.com

- Facebook (www.facebook.com)

- Twitter (www.twitter.com)

- LinkedIn (www.linkedin.com)

- Slideshare (www.slideshare.net)

- Medium (www.medium.com)

- Other Blogs (Guest Posting)

- Forums

- Instagram (www.instagram.com)

- Reddit (www.reddit.com)

- Tumblr (www.tumblr.com)

- Quora (www.quora.com)

Launch Your Very Own Radio Station

With the ever-evolving technologies these days, you CAN afford your very own radio station. Have you ever thought about being able to broadcast sharing your business growth strategy using your very own radio channel? Your radio station will do what every other radio station does. It will work as an advertising channel for your business. It will spread information about who you are and what you do and precisely what you have to offer to your prospects.

Let's take a detailed look at how it works.

Benefits

About 93 percent of the Americans who are aged 12 years old, tune in to the radio once in a week. The growth of radios due to smartphones has also been outstanding due to apps like Pandor and Spotify. Radio streaming is on a constant rise as about 54 percent of the Americans prefer online radio streaming at least once in a month. Since the year 2017, there is a 45 percent rise in this streaming[4].

The base of radio listeners is increasing by the day. Due to this, it is high time that business coaching services acknowledge the importance of radio marketing and use it regularly to achieve high-yield in their businesses.

Based on the statistics mentioned above, the following are some of the main benefits of advertising through the

---

[4] Theisen, S. (2018). 5 Ways Radio Advertising and Branding Can Benefit Your Business. Leighton Broadcasting. Retrieved from: https://blog.leightonbroadcasting.com/blog/5-ways-radio-advertising-and-branding-can-benefit-your-business

radio.

Relatively Low Cost

A radio channel doesn't cost as much as a television channel or billboard advertisement relatively.

Accessibility & Mobility

A radio channel is an effective way of promoting your business coaching services because it lets the audience listen to you quite literally. Listeners can tune in to the radio anytime and anyplace. You can create podcasts from your radio channel by requesting your listeners to ask whatever questions they intend to.

It will establish your reputation as an expert. As a result, your radio channel will not only contribute to marketing; it will also help in building you as an authority in business/marketing coaching — the effectiveness of the radio channel increases due to its dual-action.

Prestige and Reputation

When you have your radio channel, it's possible to become a renowned name in your industry. People recognize you for the advice you relay through your show. This will enable you to build a prestigious reputation for yourself in your industry. Use these resources to create your very own radio station:

Resources:
- https://live365.com/
- https://www.voscast.com/
- https://www.radiojar.com/

Use LinkedIn and Its Sales Tools

If there's any platform better than Facebook, when it comes to meeting people associated with businesses, it is LinkedIn. LinkedIn is considered a hub of professional networks where people socialize according to their professional needs. Therefore, you need to create a LinkedIn profile for your business and then market your services in a place where you are more likely to meet your potential clients. Important reminder though-don't jump to start selling your services to your network right away.

The first time, introduce yourself and briefly tell your

connection with what you do. A few days later, touch base with your connection again to see if they would like for you to share some business growth strategies. Start adding layers to your conversation with them. It may take two or three *"meetings"* with your connection before they become your paying client.

LinkedIn is now providing advertising services to its subscribers. It is a fee-based service that is available in different packages to suit your budget. If you already have an account on LinkedIn, you just have to subscribe to this advertising service.

There are three significant benefits of LinkedIn ads. These are as follows:

- You can target your audience through this feature and choose the audience to who your ads will be visible.

- You can use these ads for any number of reasons, such as creating brand awareness, hiring individuals, or even promoting the services that you provide.

- You can keep your budget under control through

LinkedIn ads. There are multiple ways of doing that. You can bid against other LinkedIn users to reach your target audiences. You also have an option to pick a package that meets your monthly budget. The only way you can do that is by setting scheduled bids for your ads or paying only for the messages that have been delivered to your audiences. In the latter option, you will only be charged for the e-mails that get delivered to your audience.

You can subscribe to LinkedIn advertising through the following link: https://business.linkedin.com/marketing-solutions/ads

Other super effective LinkedIn sales tools include:

- SalesNavigator

- Profinder:

- Linked Helper

I personally generate about 80 percent of my leads using LinkedIn sales tools. This is to the point I made earlier: Test a few strategies and settle on a few that fit you best. Many of my fellow business coaches achieved a great level of success using PPC, Click Funnels, Facebook Ads, their own radio stations, or writing articles and press releases. Try not to spread yourself thin because it might devastate you financially and emotionally.

Use Local Business Listings

Listing your business in local business directories is another excellent way to expose your services to your potential clients. You can locally list your business in platforms such as Google Places, Yellow pages, Yelp (https://www.yelp.com/), and many other similar platforms that people go to.

Stay aware of the fact that listing your business on any business listings requires a fee. Make the best pick based on your budget. Before investing in any such platform, you have to calculate your return on investment (ROI) to make sure that they benefit you for the best.

Write a Book

Writing a book is the ultimate ticket to establishing

yourself as an authority. Authors are seen as instant subject matter experts. Writing a book would enable you to attract media attention, dazzle clients and prospects, create opportunities for speaking engagements, and lots more. If you want to be an expert, make book writing a top priority for you.

Write books about your industry. Include the kind of information in your book that is comprised of your experiences. Make sure that whatever content you add to your book stays relevant to your field, and no other author has repeated it. You can publish your books on Lulu (http://www.lulu.com/), Kindle Publishing House (https://kdp.amazon.com/en_US/), Createspace (https://www.createspace.com/), and many other Websites, which are accessible easily online.

Whichever marketing strategy you choose, be sure to show the value you bring to the customer. Stating the value in your marketing messages is critically important for establishing yourself as an expert business coach and showcasing your ability to help business owners grow and generate more revenue, which is the ultimate goal of the business coaching profession.

Chapter Summary

The strategies for your business growth offered in this chapter offer enormous value if implemented consistently and with the right target audience in mind. No matter what strategy or strategies you pick, be sure to deliver the value to your prospects and stay consistent in your effort.

COACHING ASSIGNMENT #6:

Choose one or two marketing strategies from this chapter. Research more about them using the links provided. Then, determine how you can put them to use. Start implementing them. Start tracking your metrics.

Chapter 7
Help Your Customers Grow with Five of the Best Business Development Strategies

In the context of this book only, by *"prospects,"* I refer to small- to medium-size business owners, who are your target audience you will be working with.

EXPERT TIP Whichever strategy(s) you choose to recommend for your prospects, make sure you are able to enter the conversation taking place in their heads.

The *"conversation"* that is taking place in EVERY prospect's mind revolves around two major things:

1. There's a problem they have, and they don't want.
2. There's a result they want but don't have.

Your main goal as a business coach is to help your

prospects get rid of the problem they have, and they don't want AND help them achieve a result that they want but don't have.

There is a marketing formula that takes these two points into account. Once used, that marketing formula helps spit out a message so compelling it practically forces buyers to buy what your prospects (business owners) sell.

It's called the **Conversion Equation**. The Conversion Equation looks like this:

Interrupt	Engage	Educate	Offer
The **Interrupt** is the business marketing message Headline	The **Engage** is the business marketing message Sub-Headline	The **Educate** is the information business owner provides either verbally or in writing that presents evidence to prospective buyers that the product or service is the best in every way to the competition	The **Offer** MUST be so compelling and so irresistible that prospective buyers can't resist it

The **Interrupt** is the business marketing message headline: This means it's the first thing someone sees when they visit your prospect's website, read any of the business marketing collateral, or hear your prospect speak. The **Interrupt** MUST address the problem your prospects have that they don't want.

The **Engage** is the business marketing message Sub-Headline: This means it is the second thing your prospect's buyers see or hear. The **Engage** MUST address the result your prospects wants but doesn't have.

The **Educate** is the information prospects provide either verbally or in writing about their business. It provides evidence to their buyers that the prospects' product or service is the best in every way to the competition. Unfortunately, MOST businesses aren't different from their competitors, and that's why business owners MUST innovate their business to create a **market-dominating position.**

Your prospects MUST make their businesses unique. Their business MUST stand out from the crowd. It MUST make prospect's buyers say to themselves that they would be absolute idiots to buy from anyone else but your prospect – regardless of price.

And finally, the **Offer.** Your prospects MUST create a compelling offer that makes it so irresistible that their prospective buyers can't turn it down. But here's another critical fundamental of marketing. Because of the saturation of marketing messaging these days, most buyers have become numb to most marketing. Following the Conversion Equation can dramatically overcome this. However, even with this powerful tool in play, it will still take multiple points before your prospects' buyers will buy what your prospects sell.

For most businesses today, it takes anywhere from 20 to more than 100 touch points before a buyer makes their buying decision. Following the Conversion, Equation reduces the touch points to somewhere between 5 to 12 points of contact. But here's the key... most businesses don't follow up with their prospects at all, and this provides a HUGE window of opportunity for ANY business that does follow up... to position themselves as the dominant force in their industry. To have the opportunity to get your prospects' message in front of their prospective buyers 5 to 12 times, you MUST have your prospects find a way to collect their contact information, and that's the purpose of their Offer.

Most businesses offer something that only appeals to the category of buyers called *"NOW BUYERS."* In other words, buyers who are ready to make an immediate purchase. For example, if my Air Conditioner broke down in the middle of the summer, I'm ready to buy a new one this very moment. I become a *"NOW BUYER."* Unfortunately, NOW buyers make up less than 1 percent of the total number of buyers that are in the market to buy what you sell. These businesses typically offer buyers a free consultation, a discount, a coupon, a free assessment, a complimentary quote... or the biggest mistake of all... CALL US!

For most businesses, all of their marketing material... their website... their business card... all list their phone numbers as their sole offer...and that ONLY appeals to that 1 percent of *"NOW BUYERS."* The remaining 99 percent of viable buyers are *"investigating"* and gathering information about what your prospects sell. They're searching for information because they want to determine who is offering the best value. You see, prospective buyers DON'T shop price – they shop VALUE! The only reason prospective buyers consider price is that most businesses don't give them any other value proposition to consider except the price. Most businesses don't establish their **market-dominating position.** Since all of their competitors look exactly the same, prospective buyers are FORCED to shop price.

To help you better understand the **Conversion Equation,** let me give you an example of a marketing message from a Doctor of Endocrinology that applied the Conversion Equation.

- **Interrupt:** *"As someone diagnosed with Diabetes, are you struggling to gain control of your disease?"*
- **Engage:** Are you experiencing numbness in your limbs, increased urination, weight loss, increased appetite, blurry vision, itchy skin, unexplained fatigue, and thirst that seem impossible to control?
- **Educate:** My name is Dr. John Smith, and I help patients like you every day to learn the advanced treatment methods available to us that will help you control, treat, and potentially cure your diabetes to allow you to live a long, happy life.
- **Offer:** Enter your first name and e-mail in the box

to the right, and I'll send you a series of educational videos that explain how we help people like you to combat diabetes and regain control of your life successfully.

The five-step profit formula any business coach should teach their prospects consists of the following:

1. **More Leads**
2. **More Conversions**
3. **More Transactions**
4. **Higher Prices**
5. **More Profits**

Let's take a closer look at each of these strategies:

More Leads

According to Dan Kennedy, a renowned and trusted marketing advisor, the formula for generating more leads is **Market, Message, and Media**.

- **Market:** Have your coaching client define their ideal customer. Whether it is women between 20-30 years of age or parents with children, they must know to whom they are selling.

- **Message**: Have your coaching client define their best value proposition. How are they different from their competitors? What value do they bring to the customers by selling their products or services?

- **Media:** Help your coaching client decide which media would be the most appropriate for their **market**. What media would help them convey their **message** in the most cost-effective way?

Example: A childcare center I worked with got 20 leads a month running a Facebook ad ($3000K/month). Here is their original ad:

- *We cater to ages 0-5 years old.*
- *Experienced, loving teachers.*

Now, enter the conversation taking place in customers' heads: *"What I am really looking for is safety for my kid, quality care, nutritious meals, and good education."* Does this ad answer customer concerns? ABSOLUTELY NOT!

We took a look at market, message, media to revise this ad for effectiveness.

MARKET: Parents worried about their children.

MESSAGE: *"Parents, have peace of mind! Your child will be safe with our caring teachers. Our meals are home quality or better, and we GUARANTEE your child will be reading and writing in no time. We provide such a nurturing environment that your child won't even notice they left home."*

MEDIA: Facebook Pay Per Click (PPC), Targeted Direct Mail

As a result, the center started getting 200 leads per month. That's a 1000 percent lead increase. It was so successful they had to stop the ad from running.

More Conversions

In the world of marketing, *"conversions"* mean converting leads into paying customers. Strategies that help improve conversions include the following.

- **Down-Selling**. Create offers to buy products or services at a lower price.

- **Drip Campaigns.** Understand that only one percent of customers are ready to buy now. Stay in touch with customers until they are ready by keeping them up-to-date about new advances with your products or services.

- **Create Irresistible Offers.** Your coaching clients' offers must be so good that the prospects will buy without hesitation.

<u>**Example:** A</u> cosmetic surgeon I worked with specialized in *"mommy makeovers."* He was running Facebook PPC ads with a zero conversion rate and spending $3000/month. Here is his original ad:

Call us at 555-564-1223 to schedule your free consultation.

Where is the offer? There is no irresistible, compelling offer. The strategy I recommended instead:

MARKET: Women between 30-50

MESSAGE: *"Want to have the body you had two kids ago?"*

MEDIA:

- Direct Website visitors to a *"squeeze page"* or landing page versus his Website to capture visitors' contact info. He could then send them free informational materials about the procedure's risks, benefits, and share customer testimonials.

Facebook PPC:

- The new ad is now generating 200-400 <u>prospects</u> per month. The new ad's 60 percent conversion rate is now generating 240 new leads. 240 new leads result in 20 new patients monthly. This has resulted in approximately $200,000 in <u>monthly</u> revenue.

More Transactions

More transactions mean having customers buy more frequently from you. The tactics to get more transactions include:

- **Upselling or Cross-Selling:** Have your coaching clients offer their products or services at a higher price with an offer to buy a bundle.

- **Offering More Products or Services:** Have your coaching clients expand the variety of their products or services and offer them to prospects and customers.

Example: A furniture store owner who sells furniture is also offering *"free"* leather cleaning twice a year; a warranty for three years; moving and installation; home accessories, etc. They can use each furniture sale as an opportunity for additional up-sells and cross-sells. This creates the perception of adding MASSIVE value.

Another example would be a beauty salon that offers shampoos, hair conditioners, hairdryers, nail polish, etc. as additional up-sells and cross-sells to their grooming services.

Higher Prices

Suggest your coaching clients increase prices by improving the quality of the products or services they are selling. They could also bundle their products or services into a *"package."* The price increase must be based on the **true value** that they are offering at a higher price.

Example: A home security company sells home alarm system packages for $100 a month. The package includes two units in the house and the kitchen, as well as free installation. For *"only"* $50 a month more ($150 total), they are offering an upgraded bundle that includes five units and all doors and windows in the house, plus free hardware and installation. It's all about which one of these is PERCEIVED as offering the MOST VALUE.

More Profits

There are two key methods to increase your coaching client's overall profitability:

1) **Increase revenue** or

2) **Decrease their costs of doing business**

Your coaching clients can increase revenue by raising prices. They can decrease the cost of doing business by cutting labor costs. But the true factor to increasing your coaching clients' profitability is to have them offer more **value** than their competition. Prospects will pay twice the price if they believe they're receiving four times more value.

Note that most small businesses have never even considered raising their prices. They firmly believe that ANY price increase will lead to customers abandoning them.

THIS WILL **NOT** HAPPEN! A handful of customers may leave, but they are most likely your biggest price shoppers that have no respect for your business anyway.

Say a business is selling a widget for $50. You coach them to raise their prices to $60 per item. The business is now making an additional $10…**ALL of which is profit**. That's a **20 percent profit increase!**

For the business to make $1000 in profit selling their widgets at $50 each, they would need to sell 20 widgets. But by increasing the price 20 percent, they only need to sell 16.6 widgets. There simply is no **FASTER** or **EASIER** way to generate additional revenue.

The real key to increasing profitability is to **offer more value than the competition.** Unfortunately, businesses mistakenly attempt to increase their value by offering discounts that annihilate their margins.

- **Have your customer STOP discounting!**

When a business discounts their price, they lose the **full value** of <u>every</u> dollar they discount. **Innovate** the business, so they **offer more value** than their competition even if that means <u>increasing</u> their price. All these five strategies are core and fundamental to marketing **any** business. There are more strategies that you can offer to your prospects for implementation in addition to the five main ones we discussed earlier. I scrutinized more ways to help your prospects generate hundreds of thousands of dollars in the book I wrote earlier.

It is titled *"Instant Marketing Success…10 New & Radical Strategies to Help Your Business Strive."* (Elena Nugent, 2017) and it is available on <u>Amazon.</u> You will be amazed to learn how those additional methods that I presented in my *"<u>Instant Marketing Success…10 New & Radical Strategies to Help Your Business Strive</u>"* can help business owners make more money with less effort when implemented with strategy and care.

Chapter Summary:

In conclusion, if you can help your coaching clients get more leads, more conversions, more transactions and offer some strategies for raising prices and profits, they will see their business grow tremendously within the next three to six months. Help them stay their course and provide the best coaching value!

Make sure to keep these five best business development strategies in mind when communicating your value to prospective clients. Make sure to let them know exactly what you can do for them.

COACHING ASSIGNMENT #7: For practicing purposes, offer a business owner you know to have a strategy session with them to identify more revenue for their business using the methods outlined in the second part of this chapter.

Chapter 8
Use These Automation Tools to Increase Your Productivity and Improve Efficiency

For business coaches managing a daily schedule, staying efficient, and by the same token, being able to provide value to the paying customers is a Herculean task. This affects coaches' effectiveness and ability to deliver. We are blessed to live in the 21st century because it offers so many automation tools and applications for all your needs, both personal and professional.

Business coaching is no exception. I handpicked the tools that you can use to help you do more with less effort during the day. Before you settle on a few, definitely sign up for free trials if they are available. Play with those and decide for yourself what best supports your work routine and fits your budget.

Coaching Organizational Tools and Project Management:

Coaches Console

Coaches Console (https://www.coachesconsole.com/) is a one-stop solution, especially for coaches who are just starting. You can house your Website on this app, manage your calendar and e-mail list.

CoachAccountable

CoachAccountable(https://www.coachaccountable.com/) is a powerful tool for managing your clients. It can be used for tracking coaching sessions, communications, paperwork, and other coaching activities. It is also used to manage coaching groups and classes. CoachAccountable makes coaching easier through a collection of tools.

It enables you and your clients to decide on what to do and when it will be done.

It has the following features:

- Automatic reminders that keep clients on track.
- At any time, everyone can see what is done and what is not.

- The evidence of completed actions makes accomplishments real.

- It sends reminders via text or e-mail to make reporting simple.

- It enables everyone to see the scoreboard of how things are unfolding at any time.

- Its graphs tell a story about how things went and what worked.

- It enables your clients to book an appointment with your online.

- It sends reminders to ensure that everyone comes prepared and on time.

- It integrates easily with your regular calendar.

Satoriapp

This is an affordable and straightforward app that helps coaches to cater to their clients for a meager amount of money. Satoriapp (http://satoriapp.com/) also gives coaches information about how to become a successful coach online, information about how to start, grow, and streamline your online coaching business.

CoachLogix

CoachLogix (https://www.coachlogix.com/) is a secure, all-in-one, an online coaching management platform that is created and designed to monitor the progress and impact of coaching activities between you and your clients.

Acuity

Acuity (https://acuityscheduling.com/) gives you such options as calendars and the ability to send questions and forms to your clients before your sessions.

Google Drive

Google Drive (https://www.google.com/drive/) can be used in combination with Dropbox (https://www.dropbox.com/) and Calendly (https://calendly.com/). These programs integrate easily and enable your clients to access the drives remotely or on their smartphones.

Google Sheets

Google Sheets is a spreadsheet program offered by Google within its Google Drive service. It enables to collaborate on files in real time that is a huge productivity booster.

Monday.com

Monday.com is a tool that allows you to plan, track, and collaborate by seeing a big picture – all in one place.

Schedule Once

ScheduleOnce (https://www.scheduleonce.com/) is another great calendaring tool that enables you to provide a link to your calendar to your coaching clients if they want to schedule a time with you. The app allows you to customize everything about the tool, including the feel, and look for a better appeal.

Infusionsoft and AppointmentCore

Infusionsoft and AppointmentCore work together. Anytime a client books an appointment via AppointmentCore(https://www.appointmentcore.com/), it is automatically added to their record in Infusionsoft (https://www.infusionsoft.com/). Through this tool, you can monitor the clients' conversations and progress. You can record the conversations using the Notes feature of the Infusionsoft client record.

Calendly

Calendly (https://calendly.com/) is another scheduling app that allows you to customize your events. When you share it with your clients, it keeps them informed about your availability. Whenever a client books an appointment with you, it sends you an update about a new event and adds the event to your calendar. At the end of the month, if there is a need to track your client hours, you only have to search your calendar.

You Can Book Me

You Can Book Me (https://youcanbook.me/) is free scheduling software that works perfectly with Gmail and allows you to schedule across time zones. It also gives you the liberty to customize the look and the language of your booking page. You can send e-mail and text reminders for just a few dollars. The excellent customer service derivable from this app makes it a must-have for all professional business coaches.

Time Trade

TimeTrade (https://www.timetrade.com/) is a software company, which offers self-service and assisted-service appointment scheduling solutions.

TEMI

TEMI (https://www.temi.com/) is an online service provider that helps in converting audio files to text within minutes. You only need to pay a minimal amount of money, upload your audio file, and it will be transcribed and e-mailed to you in text form within minutes.

Keynote

Keynote (https://www.apple.com/lae/keynote/) is a presentation software application developed as a part of the iWork productivity suite by Apple Inc. It allows you to make amazing presentations in which anybody can collaborate.

Urlora

Urlora (https://urlora.com/) is a tool designed to increase conversions, sales, and traffic by adding branded call-to-action and retargeting pixels on every link you share. This custom link tool can certainly simplify all of your marketing efforts by creating unique audiences and getting detailed analytics from all of your links. For example, if you are already using Facebook, Google, LinkedIn, and other platforms, you can go ahead and integrate Urlora with targeting pixels from those platforms to organize your audiences that you created from various platforms.

Video Making
Animoto

Animoto is a powerful tool that you can use to take still photos and turn them into jaw-dropping videos. Whenever you need a quick video, Animoto (https://animoto.com/) is your go-to app.

Article Video Robot

Article Video Robot creates videos for you in the same way that Animoto does. The only difference is that while

Animoto creates videos from still pictures, Article Video Robot (https://www.articlevideorobot.com/) creates videos from article content only. Within five minutes, you can create a video for each article. Finally, you have your article in video format, and it can be watched on any video site.

Loom

Loom (https://www.useloom.com/) is a free, easy-to-use screen and video recording software.

Lumen5

Lumen5 is a video creation platform for business. With Lumen5 (https://lumen5.com/), you can create free videos for your blog, your social media, your business, and every other thing that requires video.

Customer Relationship Management

- **AWeber** (https://www.aweber.com/homepage.htm)

AWeber is a Website-based service that allows you to grow your mailing list, create opt-in forms, and carry out different kinds of experiments to make sure operations go as efficiently as possible.

Here are some of the highlighting features of Aweber:

- **E-mail Marketing:** It allows you to use e-mail marketing to build your brand and boost your revenue.

- **Plan E-mail Strategy:** You choose and set achievable goals that dictate your e-mail marketing strategy and bring you success.

- **Expand Your E-mail List:** It allows you to maximize your e-mail list by giving you writing tips.

- **Design Beautiful E-mails:** You learn how to create beautiful and engaging e-mails with design practices that are offered here.

- **Schedule and Send E-mails:** Learn how to schedule and send your e-mails on the best day and the best time.

- **Advanced E-mail Automation:** You can use e-mail automation to create multiple autoresponder series of e-mails, which saves you time.

- **Getresponse** (https://www.getresponse.com/)

Here are some of the highlighting features of Getresponse:

- **E-mail Marketing:** It allows you to send beautifully designed e-mails and get a positive response from the prospects.

- **Landing Pages:** Create 100 responsive landing pages and web forms by using drag and drop.

- **Marketing Automation:** You can also create marketing automation workflows by using an easy drag and drop creator to analyze subscriber behaviors in real-time.

- **CRM:** Create a pipeline to nurture your leads and turn them into repeat customers.

Blogging / Writing
FirePow

Many coaches use blogging to promote their business coaching services and also as part of add-on coaching to provide more value to their customers. FirePow (https://firepowblog.wordpress.com/) provides unprecedented blogging capabilities for the business coaches who want to share their knowledge with their subscribers. FirePow is an app you can use to manage several blogs. It can install a new blog in seconds. It keeps the blog software and add-ons updated. It can manage your posts, pages, and so on. It has an inbuilt content creator called Content Blitz that will load up the content automatically to be shown from a selected number of sources. It can bookmark your posts. It has a blog network that permits you to promote your blog and other numerous promotional tools and features, as well.

Unique Article Wizard

Unique Article Wizard (http://www.uniquearticlewizard.com/indexcb.html) is a service that re-spins your article before posting it to each new article directory. It works differently from the way a human works. It can submit articles to thousands of article sites and will only submit to those that are relevant to your article.

Web Conferencing
Instant Teleseminar

Instant Teleseminar (https://instantteleseminar.com/) is an inexpensive way to get your message to a large number of people simultaneously. It allows you to host online seminars in an online conference room that combines voice, chat, and Web surfing functions, which creates a fully interactive environment. Voice Over Internet Protocol (VOIP) Web conferencing services are the relevant services that allow you to conduct the meetings with your customers effectively and efficiently VOIP will enable you to make and receive phone calls over the Internet either at no cost or at a giveaway price.

Join.me

At join.me (https://www.join.me/), free screen sharing, online meetings, and team collaboration are all fast and easy.

Virtual Assistants

You will need to make sure you spend your time wisely by growing your business, prospecting, coaching, answering your clients' emails and inquiries, making presentations, networking, training, and others. Delegating the tasks that might just *"eat"* all of your time is critically necessary. That's why hiring virtual help would enable you to focus on more strategic tasks in support of your business. Consider these resources to hire a virtual assistant (VA).

- https://belaysolutions.com/
- https://www.answerconnect.com/
- https://www.answerforce.com/
- https://www.zirtual.com/

Web / Landing Pages Design

- **LeadPages** (https://www.leadpages.net/)

This is an online platform that helps in creating high-converting, mobile-responsive landing pages that generate interest, leads, and revenue for businesses.

Simply put, a landing page is the Web page on which

your prospects land when the click of one of your Google ads, or any other ad that you posted online to get traffic on your Website. A landing page is always only designed keeping in mind your Call-to-Action (CTA).

The CTA is the trigger that makes the visitor take action, which leads to purchasing your product or service.

LeadPages (https://www.leadpages.net/) specializes in creating landing pages for business.

Automating your business coaching is no longer a luxury but rather a necessity. If you want to stay on top of the game by managing your own time, resources, and money as well as your customer success, you must automate all essential tasks such as scheduling, project management, accounting, blog management, sales video production, and others that you think are necessary.

Chapter Summary

There are lots of automation tools out there to help us stay efficient in managing our time and business. It is important that you not overwhelm yourself with those. Research and pick the ones that fit your business style and wallet.

COACHING ASSIGNMENT #8: Identify the essential tasks that you need to automate and sign up for automation tools in support of those tasks.

Chapter 9
Establish Yourself as an Expert Authority in your Business Coaching Field

You and I have a come a long way and now that we have established all the great strategies and hopefully the automation tools that you can use to start your coaching business and maintain that success, it is time to learn a few strategies that you can use to establish your authority in the business coaching industry.

Use these strategies to help you become an expert authority in the business coaching field. Just a reminder – you **do not have** to employ all of them. Pick only a few that fit your needs, schedule, and budget and stick with them. Stay patient and consistent. Once you start monetizing the strategies you picked, move on to add others.

Form a Network with the Leaders in Your Field

If you want to be an expert in your professional game,

you must surround yourself with people who have the professional acumen that you are trying to achieve. Expertise is contagious. Spending time with experts in your field will help you in grabbing some of their wisdom. Then you can set out on the path to becoming just like them.

Be a Mentor to Someone in Your Field

When you share your knowledge with others, you revise it so many times that you become well-versed in it. Mentoring can be a difficult job when you don't have a mentee. Find a rising star in your field and be a mentor to them. Share your hard-earned knowledge with them. Keep your eyes, ears, and mind open as you will also learn from the person whom you are mentoring.

Not to mention, while mentoring, you will stay updated with the latest knowledge of your industry only because you would not want to give outdated information to your mentee.

Get a Mentor / Coach for Yourself

Nothing builds confidence like an endowed, knowledgeable individual showing you the way and patting you on the back for a job well done. An excellent and competent mentor can act as a mirror, giving you the viewpoint that you need to believe in yourself. Read on the subject of trials and tribulations of flourishing entrepreneurs. Converse together with successful business owners and ask them to elaborate on their disappointments, as well as their successes. Many internet forums endow budding entrepreneurs with such opportunities. It also gives you the ability to establish a rapport with such individuals.

Finding a mentor is crucial. You can get distracted and dissuaded when you don't have someone to guide you. However, when you can personally rely on someone who's been through the wringer and can help you achieve your goals, it's easier to stay on track with your time. Find a good mentor that can help you along your path.

Be a Thought Leader

Experts are never satisfied with the status quo. They always look for the next level of advancement in their profession. They always try new techniques, improve on existing concepts, explore new ideas, and add value to their work. They always try to push boundaries and expand the limits of their field. Experts are leading the way for the future of their profession. They do not accept the standard practice; they always question, challenge, and create new things.

Showcase Your Knowledge

Experts derive joy from demonstrating and sharing their skills and knowledge. They always want to be of help to their professional community. For you to be seen as an expert, you must put your expertise out there for everyone to benefit from. Inspire others to think differently about your profession. Be loud and bold and don't be afraid to draw attention to yourself and your point of view. Make it a duty to train others! Talk about topics of interest at a meeting of your professional association.

Stay Up-To-Date on Latest Trends

Every field changes. Change is inevitable. Some changes happen more rapidly than others. Experts are always at the forefront of such changes, exploring new trends, and trying to understand where their industry is heading. They have the foresight and are not afraid of the latest and greatest technology and innovations that challenge the tested and trusted methods of the past. Your best tool for doing this is reading. Professional publications often discuss new trends and how they are shaping the future of your industry. Your professional network is also a handy tool. Talk about the latest trends in your field and share your thoughts while you are networking within business communication.

Never Stop Learning

Your best bet for achieving expertise is always keeping an open mind and absorbing new information. Always read books, blogs, and other materials to learn new things about your industry and maintain a firm grasp on the things you already know. Take classes, both online and in-person, let your expertise spring from the expertise of others. The more you learn, the closer you get to become an expert.

Write a Book

Writing a book is the ultimate ticket to establishing yourself as an authority. Authors are seen as instant subject matter experts. This enables them to attract media attention, dazzle clients and prospects, create opportunities for speaking engagements, and lots more. If you want to be an expert, make book writing a top priority for you. Write books about your industry. Include the kind of information in your book that is comprised of your experiences. Make sure that whatever content you add to your book stays relevant to your field, and no other author has repeated it. You can publish your books on Lulu (http://www.lulu.com/), Kindle Publishing House (https://kdp.amazon.com/en_US/), Createspace (https://www.createspace.com/), and many other Websites, which are accessible easily online.

Publish Articles

Article writing allows you to share your opinions and gain exposure to a greater audience. You can write for online outlets or print media. Write for as many outlets as you can. You can either go for 500-word short articles or long 1000-word articles. You can also add keywords to your articles to attract traffic specific to your business coaching practice. EzineArticles (http://ezinearticles.com/), Hubpages (https://hubpages.com/), and eHow (https://www.ehow.com/) are the top Websites for publishing your articles and establishing your credibility as a business coach. Remember, the materials that you post on these Websites are inspected for quality, so make sure you deliver the best content you have.

Host a Blog

Blogging is a powerful tool used to connect with your audience, drive traffic to your Website, and establish yourself as an expert in your subject matter. Write new posts at least two to three times each week to achieve the best results. You can host your blog on Joomla (https://www.joomla.org/), WordPress (https://wordpress.org/), Drupal (https://www.drupal.org/), and many other blogging platforms which can give your services a massive reach!

Build a Social Media Following

Social media Websites such as Facebook, Twitter, and LinkedIn are potent tools to help you establish yourself as an expert. They afford you limitless access to an audience. Share links to your blog posts, news, quick tips, opinions, and questions on your social media page. Your followers will appreciate it a lot if they know that you appreciate them.

Create a YouTube Channel

Nowadays, when you run a search on Google for anything, the results are always dominated by YouTube videos. Get a camera and put together a series of short and engaging videos. Promote these videos on your social networks and feature them on your Website for greater exposure.

Be a Guest on Internet Radio Shows

Being a guest on the Internet Radio Show is a very powerful tool that is not being fully utilized by experts. There are numerous internet radio shows, many of which have a large following. You can find programs on everything on internet radios. On Internet radios, guests are often featured for between 15 minutes and an hour. Here are examples of internet radios you can get started with:

- http://blogtalkradio.com
- http://alltalkradio.com

- http://womensradio.com

Host Teleseminars

The Teleseminar format has been around for some time now. With a conference line and a phone, it is possible for you to host events where you can lead an educational discussion, or you can invite guests such as small business owners or other coaches to give speeches or interviews. For your teleseminars, you can make use of the following tools:

- http://instantteleseminar.com
- http://freeteleseminar.com

Host Online Events

You can take teleseminars and Webinars to a new level by conducting an entire conference online. You can invite different resource persons, charge for admission, and sell the recordings for years to come!

http://eventbrite.com is an excellent tool for managing event registration.

Refer to Yourself as an Expert

You can refer to yourself as an expert. However, a better option might be to create a catchy tagline for yourself that explains what you do. Let people know what you have to offer, and this messaging should be consistent across your Website, social media profiles, business cards, marketing collateral, you name it!

Become an Influencer

You can become an influential leader in your field in many ways. For instance, you can volunteer to serve with a related trade organization. You can also start your group in person or online. Becoming a leader is an effective way of establishing yourself as an expert.

Create and Distribute Informational Products

Based on your knowledge, you can create products such as white papers, e-books, special reports, workbooks, podcasts, or videos. Then, you can either give them away for promotional purposes or sell them. Through this, buyers will identify you as an authority in your field. This can also lead to other opportunities, such as coaching offers or speaking engagements.

Form Strategic Alliances

You can reach a bigger audience by connecting with others who have already reached your audience and find ways of working together. When somebody else introduces you to their networks, that endorsement can lead to people registering for your services immediately. You can cross-promote each other in your newsletters, co-sponsor an event, or just agree to send referrals to each other.

Teach Classes and Workshops

Not only is teaching a powerful way to establish your authority, but it can also be incredibly rewarding. You are setting yourself up as an expert when you teach in classes, or you host workshops at your own office.

Set Yourself Apart from Your Competition

Consider what makes you unique and then figure out how to build that into your overall brand. Challenge yourself to tackle one new tactic each month. By doing so, you will establish yourself as an expert in your chosen field.

Maintain Smart Online Profile

Make your online profile very attractive. Find industry blogs and forums and start posting comments that bring value to other coaches and small business owners.

Become an Active Member in a Professional Association

This implies doing more than just paying dues and attending meetings. Find a way to help. You can organize expert speakers in your field to be on a panel. It will enhance your resume, increase your self-esteem, and give you valuable connections. By doing so, you are building up relationships with people who are going to hire you.

Focus on One Subject at a Time

Don't clutter your mind with too many subject matters at the same time. Focus on one subject at a time. Do not set yourself up for failure by overwhelming yourself, learning too many things at the same time. Learn one thing at a time. When you have mastered one thing, you can proceed to learn other things one after the other.

Before you know it, you will become an expert. With time every single job you undertake will become easier than before. Due to growth in your knowledge, your personal development will pace up, and you will have an answer for just about any business-related issue.

Use Trust Triggers

After being a guest on a radio show, have spoken alongside a reputable speaker, or have had your work published by a trusted outlet, you can build trust by sharing that experience. Establishing trust triggers is vital as your audience will only stay with you when they trust you.

Project Confidence and Carry Yourself with Poise

The importance of projecting confidence when presenting your ideas in a group setting or face-to-face with the potential customer, selling on your package options, explaining the benefits of your services to the customer, is quite high. When you show yourself as the one being confident and in control, you can create an authoritative personality for yourself.

Use the following key points to maintain your confidence while addressing an audience.

- Make sure you rehearsed your answers to all possible questions relating to your offer.
- Be sure not to be overly pushy or *"sales-y."*
- Be sure to always provide the answer (even if you don't know the exact solution) to your potential customer. You will lose momentum if you say something like, *"I'm not sure. Let me get back to you on that."*
- Be positive and smile.
- State the benefits of your service to the customer with confidence.
- Don't humiliate the potential customer by providing negative feedback about their marketing strategies or Websites. Always stress the positives of what they are already doing, but be sure to emphasize the fact that they would benefit greatly from your

services.

- Make sure you do look like a business coach by dressing professionally. Nobody wants to see a guy in a flannel shirt and jeans or a girl in khaki pants trying to give business advice unless you have mutually agreed to meet informally.

- Choose your words wisely. They can either win you a deal or ruin your reputation.

- Don't try to please everyone or attend to all business sizes. Remember, your goal is to coach qualified leads. In other words, customers who have the financial means and desire to be coached to make their business are more successful in generating more revenue.

- Mind your body language. Don't use your hands too much. Keep your gestures in check. Don't fret. Just calm down and stay in a convincing demeanor.

Chapter Summary

Becoming an authority is the ultimate goal of every business coach. With becoming an authority in your field comes more coaching clients, more speaking engagements, reputation, and trusted relationships with your clients and fellow coaches. So, aim at becoming that ultimate authority in your coaching field to be successful and deliver the best value for your customers.

Coaching Assignment #9:

Identify one or two methods that would help you establish yourself as an authority in business coaching. Start implementing them. Stick with them until you are ready to add other methods.

Chapter 10
Learn How to Transition to Business Coaching Full-Time

Many aspiring coaches who still have their day jobs have a dilemma – how to transition to business coaching full-time? Starting your business coaching practice while working 9-to-5 is a challenging prospect. You almost always end up overworking. However, resigning from your regular job is not a good option when just beginning your career in business coaching. So, the question that arises here is, how do you transition from your job to business coaching smoothly? The two-step process below explains how to do so painlessly.

Step 1

Learn how to be a business coach. Visit the online business academy at www.resultsorientedcoaching.com and sign up for business coaching training. This is state of the art business academy that would teach you how to become a business coach and equip you with all the tools you need to succeed in business coaching.

Step 2

While working your day job, start conducting Marketing Bootcamps at least once monthly. These can be done early in the morning before you start your regular job, so there will be no interference. Marketing Bootcamps are a proven way of booking coaching clients and quickly building your clientele. Once you fill up your schedule with paying customers, go ahead and sever ties with your employer.

Step 3

Start offering coaching sessions after hours or weekends. Business owners are hard to catch during the day anyway because they are busy taking care of their businesses. Convincing them to take an hour out of their busy schedule during the day for coaching may not be that attractive to them. So, start small by offering the after-hours sessions, lunchtime sessions, or weekends. I found that method extremely workable for me when I just started out.

Have Clarity and Dream Big!

Coaching Assignment #10:

If you are contemplating the transition to business coaching full time, start planning the transition by offering your coaching sessions after hours and on the weekends.

Chapter 11
Learn the Words of Wisdom to Help You Move Forward Without Fear or Hesitation

Let's take a look at some of the biggest hurdles you will ever come across and how you can remove them from your path to unprecedented success in your business coaching service.

Hurdle # 1: Lack of Self-Confidence

Self-confidence implies believing in your worth as well as your chance of succeeding. It is a primary weapon for those who excel in business. When a person shows a lack of confidence, it leads others to believe the same about them. This can be seriously detrimental to a business.

Confidence is an essential building block in a flourishing career, and grasping it fully will take you places you never considered achievable. However, it doesn't develop overnight. You have to take steps in an appropriate direction and make targeted efforts to become more confident and even an unfathomably extra confident self of yours.

Why is self-confidence so important?

Confident business owners know that by being confident, one can successfully deal with clients, plan strategies, execute policies, and make decisions. Hence people trust them, value their opinions, and rely on their judgment.

Having confidence implies comprehending the value you offer and your capabilities. You can successfully communicate well as you present yourself, which consequently results in getting taken note of for all the desirable reasons and escalating your income.

How can you gain more self-confidence in business coaching?

Following are some of the firmly established strategies to get you there if you have just started your business coaching service.

Evaluate Yourself

Your confidence is your own to build up or undermine.

Believe in yourself, your aspirations, and your abilities. Keep your head high, feet on the ground, and *Believe You Can Do It*. Read a motivational story or two to uplift your spirit. Educate yourself not to be scared of failure. Understand that failure and disappointments are inescapable. They will only build and make you stronger. Fear of failure can be a tremendous blow to your self-confidence. It stops you from taking risks and attempting new things in your career.

Fortify and hone your skillsets. If there are weaknesses in them, discover ways to minimize their negative impact. Look back at places where you have gotten awards and honors or recognition for your precedent hard works and let them be an encouragement and heartbeat to your achievement on this new endeavor.

Stay Away from Negativity and Bring on Positivity

You need to assess your inner circle, including associates and relatives. Think about getting away from those people who put you down and rip up your confidence. This will create an enormous difference and help you make strides toward more self-confidence.

Change how you view yourself, assert yourself, and believe you can. Be optimistic, even if you're not feeling it quite yet. Bring to an end focusing on the struggles in your life and instead focus on solutions and make positive changes.

Focus on Planning and Preparation

People often feel less confident about new or potentially stressful situations. The most critical factor in developing confidence is planning and preparing for the unknown. If you are applying for a new job, for example, you would be wise to prepare for the interview. Plan what you would want to say in the interview and think about some of the questions that the interviewer may ask you. Practice your answers with friends or colleagues and gain their feedback.

Continue to Gain Learning, Knowledge, and Training

Learning and making inquiries can help us in feeling more confident regarding our ability to come to grips with situations, roles, and tasks. Knowing what to look forward to and how and why things are done will add to your knowledge and frequently make you more confident. This is the reason that learning, acquiring knowledge, and getting training is considered as a life-long process.

Hurdle # 2: Lack of Self-Discipline

Self-discipline is one of the most crucial skills for everyone to possess. This skill is essential in every area of life, and though most people acknowledge its importance, very few do something to strengthen it.

Self-discipline gives you the power to stick to your decisions and follow them through. It helps you persevere with your choices and plans without changing your mind until you accomplish them. Contrary to common belief, self-discipline does not mean being harsh toward yourself or living a limited, restrictive lifestyle. Self-discipline means self-control, which is a control of yourself, your actions, and your reactions.

Self-discipline is not easy for most of us. However, it is a skill that you can develop over time. However, it takes constant work and focuses on getting better, and the only way to improve your self-discipline is through intentional and dedicated practice. As with all types of self-improvement, change is difficult, and it takes time. Here are strategies to increase your self-discipline:

Get Organized

On the way to being self-disciplined and realizing your goals, you have to be organized. An organized lifestyle portrays a disciplined life. Execute one small thing a day to improve and perfect your organization. That's all it takes. Set a time limit for specific milestones. Decide on a realistic period and put in writing the date when you would like to achieve it. Successful business owners are habitually hard-driving and exceedingly focused on identifiable goals.

Manage Your Time Effectively

Being an entrepreneur, you more or less have no choice but to manage your time efficiently. It would be virtually impracticable for you to get anything done if you fail to manage your time. Our knack for self-discipline is, to a great extent, determined by our ability to manage our time effectively. The well-known time managers of the world are as well as some of the most successful individuals in their respective fields. Do away with distractions that can incapacitate productivity. Eliminate them. Set times to make calls, answer personal e-mails, or check social media.

Make a To-Do List

A significant part of self-discipline is understanding what you need to do and then doing it. When you're not used to behaving in a disciplined manner, you will sometimes find it challenging to come up with your next activity. Begin your day with a list of tasks that you need to get done. You can make the tasks work-related or schedule part of your day for personal items.

Establish a Clear Plan

You don't just wake up one day suddenly blessed with self-discipline. Instead, it would be best if you devised a strategy. You must increase your good habits and eliminate bad ones. You'll need to develop a plan to outline action steps that will help you in reaching your goals.

Hurdle # 3: Lack of Motivation

Most of the time, when entrepreneurs make the bold

leap from being an employee of a corporation to becoming the leader of their own business, one of the first challenges they face is no longer having someone above them to set goals, deadlines, and incentives. The responsibility of inspiration becomes a task of self-motivation. This can be a challenge for many, especially when the experience is new. So, how does an entrepreneur stay motivated to become a better person and business leader?

Start with Setting a Personal Mission Statement

When you start your own business, and you go down the path taken not so often, the road becomes very foggy sometimes. It's difficult to see what's ahead. Having a clear understanding of what you want to accomplish personally and how you will achieve will be required.

You must determine, what's that profound, core reason why you want to start a business? Take the time to recognize what you're trying to fulfill is because that's the root of everything that you'll do moving forward. Clarify the importance of your objectives. Whenever you catch yourself losing motivation, go back to your *"why"* and remind yourself of the reason behind what you're doing.

Keep reminding yourself of the purpose for which you became an entrepreneur.

Find a Support Group

Hang out with people who make you want to *"do"* and *"be"* better. Having someone there to encourage you, support you when things don't go as expected, and challenge you can be an effective way to stay motivated. When you commit to someone else to do something, you're no longer struggling along on your own.

You have someone else counting on you, and most of us feel increased motivation to act when there is a chance we will disappoint someone other than ourselves. Spend time appreciating the drive and determination of others, and explore how they overcame the challenges they faced on their journeys. Also, minimize contact with negative people

Despite how self-motivated you are, you'll run out of fuel eventually, so it's comforting to know you have other people whom you can fall back on. Engage your friends and colleagues to help motivate you both toward individual and shared goals.

Indulge in Inspirational Activities and Stay Positive

Watch a TED talk or listen to an inspirational podcast. Read a positive book. Listen to an audiobook or podcast with a positive message.

Set Rewards

We are naturally wired to react to incentives, so be prepared to reward yourself for accomplishing a goal or maintaining a habit. Just like in business, recognize and reward small victories along the way to long-term, broader goals.

Relive Past Successes

Do you remember what it felt like to reach an accomplishment, hit a significant milestone, or make an important decision? Spend some time thinking about the process you went through, the work you put in, and the taste of victory. Reliving some of your best moments can get you over the hurdle and into action.

Try a New Approach

Routines can bring boredom, and boredom can cause a

loss of motivation. If your habits are causing you to lose your fire, shake things up! Try altering the way you do things, when you do them, how you do them, and even how you think about them. Start to question your standard processes, and introduce a new way of thinking to get past complacency and renew your motivation.

Hurdle # 4: Lack of Public Speaking Skills

Think of the best speaker you've ever seen. They were not always that good. They struggled, they learned, they honed their craft. They become a great speaker. They weren't born that way. When they were born, I can assure you they couldn't speak at all. If you genuinely want to overcome your fear of speaking, the following tips will help you do it.

The first thing I want you to know about public speaking is that it is not a unique talent. It is a skill that you can learn and master with practice.

Build Confidence by Gradually Increasing Your Exposure

It helps if you can build your capabilities up with small doses of public speaking. This speaking can take place in your living room with five people, on a conference call, as part of a group meeting, or online through a Webinar. Starting in one of these environments, whichever one makes you feel the most at ease, is a great first step to overcoming your fear.

Other things you might try to build up your tenacity – Talk to strangers on the street, or Be Yourself.

Be Yourself!

Know your content and be comfortable with your delivery, but avoid getting locked into reading off a prepared script. You know what you're going to say and you know it's worth hearing. This won't derail you. You've got this! They showed up to listen to you specifically, and they're interested in what you have to say and didn't come to heckle you.

Do not try to memorize the content. Know your material backward and forwards but build an outline of your speech in your head and speak around that. In case you forget something – just move on. Only you know you forgot something. If you try to recollect the forgotten piece, you may lose confidence, and the audience will get distracted while you try to remember it.

Take A Public Speaking Class

I hate to regret more than anything. I'd rather fail or make a fool of myself rather than not do something I know I want to do. Taking a course or some kind of commitment that forces you to practice is a great idea.

Hurdle # 5: Too Many Distractions

Seldom does success come easily in business. Not to be pessimistic, but most entrepreneurs who make it have inevitably faced a myriad of challenges along the way. That's just the way it is.

Moreover, what has stunted their growth and success along the way hasn't necessarily been major obstacles or turbulent storms. It's been the distractions that they've allowed to invade their lives. These are often subtle overlooked distractions.

When you recognize some of the biggest distractions that plague entrepreneurs, you will be less likely to fall victim to them. Instead, you can just keep your eyes on your goals and accomplish more with less wasted effort. The key to moving forward is keeping some of the most common distractions from infiltrating any further. The following are some that I've personally experienced.

Listening to Too Many People

Most often, you'll see an otherwise intelligent, ambitious, and driven entrepreneur with a seemingly infinite number of great ideas allowing his or her vision to become clouded by listening to everyone else's opinion. It's often the catalyst for self-doubt. When you've got too many voices in your head telling you what's right and what's wrong, your inner beacon of light cannot shine.

All of a sudden, you're second-guessing yourself, and your decision-making becomes hazy. That's why I recommend getting opinions and feedback from just a few select people whom you trust and know that they have your best interests at heart.

Letting Socialization Get in the Way of Your Work

Notify friends that you do have work hours, even if you are at home. Most friends will pop over at all times of the day whenever they were free! Please make sure you are assertive and tell them what your hours of work are and that you stick to a no-visit schedule during these times. Minimize online distractions; avoid these distractions by restricting the amount of time you can spend on them. From using a timer to setting limits on how long you'll be online to using tools that shave off the hours you spend on social networking, you have many resources that you can use.

Hurdle # 6: Falling into Despair

When things seem to have gone wrong, when things don't seem to be working out for you, you will undoubtedly want to give up. Don't give in easily. You only need to find a way to fight back. What do you do to find happiness again? Let's find out.

Remember That All Things Must Pass

Whether you are living in good times or bad times, nothing ever stays the same. A run of bad luck can't go on forever. The tide will come back in; it always does. It's the law of life. Until then, keep breathing. There is light at the end of the tunnel, you may not see it today, you may not see it tomorrow, but you have to look for it, and you will surely find it when you do start looking.

Nothing Goes Right All the Time

Sometimes, clients will ask for refunds, or they won't be happy with what you provide, or the universe creates a circumstance you had no way of predicting, which you just have to deal with. In such cases, remember that not all situations will always be ideal.

Connect with Happy People

We become the people we spend the most time with, so select your circle carefully. Surround yourself with inspiring and happy people. Eliminate negative people from your life who are giving you a difficult time.

Hurdle # 7: Getting Stuck

It happens even to the best and highly motivated people among us. You sit down at your desk, and you don't know what to do. Should you start developing that new service you've been thinking about? What would be the best investment of your time? What if you don't feel like doing anything anymore, or you feel like you've just been spinning your wheels and not making any progress?

Everyone gets stuck. It's part of life. However, getting stuck can be especially dangerous when you work for and by yourself. As entrepreneurs who are responsible for your workflow and process, it is essential for you to be particularly resourceful when it comes to getting UNSTUCK. The following are a few of the tactics that you can utilize to get unstuck:

Change Your Perspective

Creativity is key to removing blocks in your working process. The worst thing you can do when feeling stuck is to sit and stare at your computer or papers. Take 10 minutes off and change your perspective - doodle, lie down on a couch or floor and meditate, go for a walk. Do whatever it takes to get a perspective.

Lose Your Fear of Getting It Wrong

Sometimes the problem with most of us is that we are

afraid to get it wrong. We are too busy trying to formulate a compelling strategy or flawless opening line. Some ideas will sound crazy to you, but won't let you go. Give them a shot. When you give your ideas a fair shot, you lose the fear of failure. Consequently, you will develop a fearless attitude to try just about anything. It will help you in getting unstuck.

Stop Aiming for Perfection

Perfectionism is just a form of garden-variety procrastination. (Any true perfectionist will find that reframe deeply confronting.) Perfectionism is a story we hide behind because putting yourself out there can be anxiety-inducing. When aiming for the perfect outcome, you may deviate from the task at hand. So, instead of trying to get the ideal results, aim to get your desired results, even if they have some flaws.

Work with a Mentor or Coach

When you run out of ideas, you need an experienced mind working with you. In business coaching services, there is only so much you can do on your own. To get unstuck, work with a mentor or coach. They can give you great advice based on their experience.

Hurdle # 8: Fear of Leadership

Entrepreneurship demands effective leadership. You need to be able to make reliable decisions, organize plans, hire teammates and provide direction -- all under the steady pressure of being accountable for all decisions and actions that you take. While working under such pressure, it's natural to develop worries and fears. Don't feel can intimidate of leadership responsibilities.

Feeling afraid of leading can obscure your judgment, render your decisions less logical, and your approach less systematic. If you want to be an effective leader, there are some fears in particular that you'll need to overcome like the fear of making wrong decisions, the fear of being criticized for your approach, the fear of speaking as an authority, the fear of accountability, the fear of failure and lots more.

You're the director, decision-maker, and figurehead for

the group. The moment you let a specific fear -- even a rational one -- enter your head and get in the way of your responsibilities, your effectiveness is going to plummet. Overcoming those fears isn't easy, but it's certainly possible, and it's necessary if you want to become or remain a great leader. Let's see how you can overcome the fear of leadership.

Embrace the Fact That You Have a Team to Lead

As a business coaching service, you have a coaching business to lead and direct. In this case, you are responsible for making major decisions, but you have to make all calls based on the fact that the business coach you will be coaching may have their ideas. Taking input from them and not taking abrupt and authoritative decisions is the key to embracing the meaning of a true leader or coach.

Acknowledge That Failing Doesn't Make You a Failure

As a leader and an entrepreneur, it can feel like the world is resting on your shoulders. Moreover, with so much riding on your decisions, failing is a tough pill to swallow.

However, the truth is that everyone fails at one point or another. Ask any successful entrepreneur, how many times they've failed, and you'll get a good laugh out of them. It's not about failing; it's about what you do as a result of that failure that determines your future. Failure is inevitable. When you make mistakes, own them and let the team know what you are going to do starting today to the right the ship. Be as prepared as you possibly can be and make adjustments along the way.

Hurdle # 9: Fear of Success

Success is not a destination. It's a journey, and it's important that we take each step feeling grounded and balanced. Spend time with your loved ones, enjoy your hobby, or follow your passion, take care of your health, and grow spiritually. This is the meaning of real success, the one that you can achieve only in balance.

Many business coaches feel afraid of success because they feel that it will not leave any time for their personal lives. However, this fear of success becomes somewhat irrelevant when the definition of success changes.

Let's see how you can get over the fear of success.

Maintain a Schedule

A proper schedule keeps your time at work limited. When you follow each of your appointments properly, you seldom compromise your commitments to meet your professional goals. As a result, your business stays successful without giving you pain.

Reframe Your Definition of Failure

The fear of success is often a disguise for fear of failure. To attempt success, you have to put yourself at risk of falling on your face. However, if you view failure as a stepping stone to success, then there's nothing to fear. Failure is evidence that you've taken action and attempted a challenge. It also provides an opportunity for learning and growing, providing the information you can use for your next success.

Work on Learning to Delegate Your Responsibilities

The more you delegate, the more time you'll have for high-level decision-making and important, money-making tasks. When you can focus on those without distraction, you can get them done faster, and you'll have more free time to spend with family and friends than you've ever had before. Your fear of success will curtail in this way, and you will see progress as a regular everyday thing. The hurdles I have listed down in this chapter may take one form or another and make your business coaching career more or less a challenge for you to manage. You must work on removing these hurdles on the path to continuous growth in your business coaching service!

Chapter Summary

I commend you on your decision to start your very own business coaching company! Your fears and hesitation are natural, and you should just observe and acknowledge them without letting them guide and control you in your decision-making.

Just start implementing small changes consistently and incrementally first on a monthly, bimonthly, then weekly basis. This will result in large differences at a later stage, also known as a *"butterfly effect."*

Coaching Assignment #11:

Decide which of all the hurdles that prevent you from moving forward can be eliminated immediately. Go ahead and remove it today! Once you have done that, evaluate another one and remove it the next week. Aim at removing one hurdle a week. If that is still challenging, give yourself a little bit of slack by removing one hurdle every two weeks. Stick with your changes.

Chapter 12
Learn the Top Three Secrets of Highly Successful Business Coaches to Break Through

Business coaching is a challenging profession that not everyone is capable of taking on. You think you have what it takes to become successful in this field, but you're mistaken. That is unless, of course, you learn the ultimate secrets to success in this field. When you have your business up and running, and success doesn't seem like a distant relative, it is time for you to take the next step and reach out to even higher levels of prosperity. I am sharing with you the Top 3 secrets that highly successful business coaches have been following for many years.

Secret #1 – Commit 100 Percent

You need to completely commit yourself to this profession and filter out all the distractions from your life. Let's look at some of the things you can do to make a 100 percent commitment to your job.

Accept Fears and Move On

Fear is etched in human nature, and it amplifies whenever a person decides to try something new in life. The fear of failing can be quite daunting, and most people give out because of it. You need to accept it and move on; otherwise, it will become a massive obstacle in your path.

I have prepared this four-step process that will help you get rid of your fear:

Acknowledge It

You need to confront your fear and acknowledge its existence. Running away from it will only make things difficult.

Embrace It

After facing your fear, you need to embrace it with open arms. If you are afraid that you might fail badly in the process of starting your business, then think about how you would feel after that happens.

Accept It

It would help if you accepted your fear as a part of the reality that can't be ignored. Admitting your fears will significantly reduce your suffering and help you prepare for any eventuality in the future.

Celebrate

After accepting your fear and acknowledging its existence, you are destined to get over it. Once you do that, you need to celebrate your victory so that you are motivated to face your other fears in life in the same way.

Mute Your Personal Social Media

Another major hurdle that you need to hop over to become a successful business coach is your time wasted on the internet, particularly on social media platforms.

Social media platforms are great for marketing uses. However, you need to avoid using them for your personal use. Cutting social media from your life will grant you the much-needed free time that you can utilize to develop yourself into a great business/marketing coach.

Don't Let Rejections Put You Down

Prepare yourself for all the rejections that you are going to get in the initial stages of your business coaching. One hundred percent commitment means staying devoted even in the face of rejections and problems. No one will purchase your services after just one pitch, and you are more likely to face more rejections than acceptance. Some people get frustrated and sad due to these periodic rejections and eventually give up. Therefore, you need to stay strong and disregard these rejections.

To be successful, you only require ten influential customers, and you will eventually find them through hard work and dedication. You need to look out for businesses that are willing to expand and avoid lazy ones who don't want growth at all.

Secret#2: Think and Act Like an Entrepreneur

Entrepreneurs work for themselves and know how to promote their business to their target audience. Since your business is about your services as a business coach, you will be required to apply all the principles of business promotion techniques on yourself. Let's take a look at a few ways you can adapt to the personality of an entrepreneur.

Don't Overthink It

Overthinking can ruin everything. It is good to be cautious about everything to execute your tasks perfectly; never let it get over your head.

Overthinking can alter your judgments and elevate your stress levels. You may start thinking negatively a lot, which can be a massive problem in the process of your business development.

Despite so many adverse effects, overthinking is quite common among many people, and not many of them know how to suppress it.

I, sometimes, as well go through overthinking. However, I can inhibit negative thoughts using the methods listed below:

- **Awareness:** Before you even begin to eliminate overthinking from your life, be aware when overthinking occurs. Look for signs such as anxiety, stress, or whenever you doubt yourself.

- **Distract yourself:** Distracting yourself into happiness can help a lot. You can start doing things that usually improve your mood, such as working out, hanging out with friends, watching a movie, etc.

- **Be grateful:** Be grateful for what you have and how fortunate you are to have the things that might be a dream of some people. This positivity will provide you immense satisfaction, and you will start appreciating your blessings.

Act Swiftly and Confidently

Confidence will take you places that you have never been before. Careers fall and rise based on how confident the person is. Belief is one of the most highlighted qualities that hiring managers look for in an interviewee. People with sky-high confidence always go the distance in life.

Confidence is the key to a great career, especially for marketing and business coaches. Some people are born with confidence, while others have to work hard to achieve it.

If you are wondering how to boost your confidence, then I have some tips for you:

- **Stand tall:** Your body language also oozes confidence if you are standing tall and straight.

- **Maintain eye contact:** Confident people always look at others in the eye whenever they are talking to them.

- **Talk slowly and clearly:** Talking slowly gives you enough time to think before you speak. Therefore, you are much less likely to say something that a leader or a coach shouldn't.

- **Use your hands in conversations:** People with a lack of confidence will always hide their hands in a discussion. Using your hand gestures during a conversation shows your confidence through body language.

Always Keep an Eye on the Prize

No matter what happens on your path towards becoming a successful business/marketing coach, keep your focus on achieving your goal. In this way, all your distractions, frustrations, and failures will vanish because you will have a clear vision of why you are doing all of this.

Admit the Fact That Setbacks Happen

You need to understand that life is full of difficulties, and you are never going to ace everything in the first go. Setbacks, big or small, are going to occur, and you need to acknowledge this fact.

Entrepreneurs go through many struggles before they finally taste success. Some of the most successful people in the world, such as Bill Gates, Elon Musk, and Jeff Bezos, went through dozens of sleepless nights and tons of failure before they made it big. Therefore, you need to address all your setbacks and understand that they are just some hurdles in your way that you need to hop over.

Have a Vision and a Plan

One of the things that entrepreneurs tend to do is create a perfect vision for their business, along with an impeccable plan to reach this vision. As a business coach, you also need to create a vision for yourself. For example, if you are starting with small businesses, then you can develop a vision to be working with medium-sized or big companies in the next five years.

Of course, creating a vision is an easy phase. Creating a plan and acting on it is what matters. Therefore, you need to work extensively on creating the plan and then implementing it strategically.

Secret#3 – Take Action and Be Ready for Success

Thinking about becoming a successful business coach and making it happen in reality are two entirely different things. You must have the capacity to take swift action. Overthinking and delay in decision-making will prove to be the worst enemies in your business coaching service.

You must be bold and confident when working as a business coach. It would help if you created a self-belief that you are an expert and know everything regarding how the business works. There is a reason why companies are opting for your services. They believe you are the right person to lead them to success. You have to express the same confidence in yourself.

Keep Your Marketing Efforts High

The next important thing you need to do is sharpen your marketing skills to promote your services. Attract as many clients as possible to increase your business. For this promotion, you need to have smart marketing skills, networking skills, selling proposition, and social proof.

When it comes to marketing efforts, you need to keep your focus on the big picture rather than small things that we do regularly, such as sending out marketing e-mails to your already stored database.

The following are some of the tips that I use to get the most out of marketing efforts:

Figure Out Your "Why"

People don't just buy what you do; they often buy why you are doing it. Determine why you want to provide services as a business coach. Your 'why' will attract business coaches to your services.

Stay Consistent

Consistency is key when it comes to marketing efforts. Your target audience needs to recognize you wherever they see you (or your brand). Consistently promote your brand through messaging and make sure that the custom messages are spell-checked.

Stay Available on Social Media Platforms That Your Potential Customers Use

The world of social media is just enormous, and it is getting bigger and bigger every single day. There are many social media platforms to choose from today. However, you don't need to utilize all of them. Instead, focus only on those where your target audience is in high concentration. Make sure to create accounts on these social media platforms so that your clients can stay in touch with you.

The success of your business coaching service depends on the time and effort you put into it. Use my guide to build a coaching brand that lasts for a lifetime.

Chapter Summary

It takes time to create great things. Success is 5 percent of good luck and 95 percent of effort and dedication. Start with a commitment to launch your very own successful business coaching practice. Afraid? Hell Yes! Who doesn't! Brush off all your fears. If you can't, just go ahead and accept them. Get into that wonderful, freedom, and wealth smelling entrepreneurial spirit and start taking actionable steps toward your goal. Once you have started, make sure you don't drop the ball and keep your eyes on the prize. Your success will follow.

Coaching Assignment #12

Work on your game plan. Start with a simple business plan for your business: Spread the numbers for your living expenses, marketing/promotion, and other business expenses. Remember: You always have an option to start part-time with this business.

Chapter 13
Ascend to Even Greater Success

Ready to Move Forward?

You are already on the right track of starting and expanding your business coaching service. If you are ready to move forward toward a successful, financially, and morally rewarding career, contact me at info@resultsch.com to request a FREE 30-minute coaching session to get more clarity.

As my BIG Thank You for buying and reading this book, I'm offering **RIGHT NOW**

a **FREE** One FULL Month OF Coaching Sessions with me to provide clarity and vision (two 30-minute sessions (**$1000 Value**). To schedule your breakthrough coaching session, go to http://resultsorientedcoaching.com/ and click the orange **Schedule an Appointment** button on the right.

I look forward to helping you thrive!

Dedicated to your business success!

Elena

Made in the USA
Middletown, DE
20 January 2020